T

How Paul Robeson Saved My Life

and Other Mostly Happy Stories

Books by Carl Reiner

Enter Laughing

All Kinds of Love

Continue Laughing

The 2000 Year Old Man in the Year 2000
(with Mel Brooks)

*How Paul Robeson Saved My Life
and Other Mostly Happy Stories*

How Paul Robeson Saved My Life

and Other Mostly Happy Stories

CARL REINER

Cliff Street Books
An Imprint of HarperCollins*Publishers*

HarperCollins books may be purchased for educational, business, or sales promotional use. For information please write: Special Markets Department, HarperCollins Publishers, Inc., 10 East 53rd Street, New York, NY 10022.

FIRST EDITION

Designed by Robin Arzt

Library of Congress Cataloging-in-Publication Data

Reiner, Carl, 1922–
    How Paul Robeson saved my life and other mostly happy stories / Carl Reiner. — 1st ed.
        p.   cm.
    ISBN 0-06-019451-0
    1. Humorous stories, American. I. Title.
PS3568.E4863H6 1999
813'.54—dc21   99-31107

99 00 01 02 03 ❖/RRD 10 9 8 7 6 5 4 3 2 1

For Jake, Nick, Livia, and Romy

Contents

Acknowledgements

My thanks to George Shapiro, Dan Strone, Barbara Scher, and Diane Reverand for doing all the things they do to help me to do what I do.

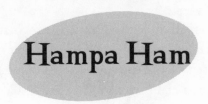

Hampa Ham

EVERY SUNDAY from the age of one, Corey Hammersberg-Carter and his parents drove from their modest home in Larchmont, New York, to Grandfather Charles Hammersberg's rolling, green estate in Holly Hill, Connecticut. At the weekly family dinner, Corey, starting at age two, addressed his maternal grandfather Hammersberg as "Hampa Ham." The old man found it terribly amusing and laughed uproariously every time Corey referred to him as Hampa Ham. He enjoyed it so much that he insisted all his grandchildren address him that way. The older ones balked, complaining that it was babyish. They were quickly reminded by their parents that Grandpa was very old and very wealthy and it was in their best interests to call their grandfather whatever he wished to be called.

Corey recalled few things about these Sunday rituals except that he didn't like the food, his cousins, or sitting at the dinner table and listening to the same inspirational speech his grandfather insisted on delivering before dessert was served. It seemed like the chocolate cake and vanilla ice cream were given as payment for sitting through the tedious, seven-and-one-half-minute lecture.

When he was eight, to fight boredom, Corey started timing the speech with the stopwatch his grandfather had given him for Christmas. The speech at its shortest was seven minutes and thirty seconds. Each week, Corey would try to guess just how many seconds under or over it would be. As the years went on, the speech took longer and longer to deliver. By the time Corey was fifteen, the speech ran close to nine minutes. Corey knew the speech backward and forward and had once recited it backward to his shocked and furious parents. They withheld his allowance for two weeks and forbade him to do it again. "Ever! Anywhere!"

Corey had learned early on that his grandfather was a multi-multimillionaire and that all his relatives, including his father, were after his money. On the Sundays when they visited the old man, his father would insist that his mother wear her most attractive clothes.

"Cynthia, darling," he remembered his father saying, "why don't you wear your darker lipstick, it enhances your smile."

When Paul Carter had asked Mr. Hammersberg for the hand of his youngest daughter, Cynthia, he had received permission and an admonition. "I will know by the bloom on my daughter's cheeks and the smile on her lips just how loving and caring a husband you are."

From that day forward, Paul was careful not to do anything that would keep his wife's lips from smiling or her cheeks from blooming. It was fortunate he liked her well enough so that being a good and thoughtful husband was not too much of a burden.

At his eighty-fifth birthday party, Hampa Ham, who had not delivered his famed "Hammersberg Address" for five years, decided once again to bore his loyal family, but with a slower, muted version.

Corey, who could still recite it backward, found himself paying rapt attention. The speech, because of the old man's infirmities, timed out at nineteen minutes, but the salient points were all there.

"Know what you want and go after it!"

"Timidity will get you nowhere."

"People who are afraid to ask questions are people who live in the dark."

"If there is someone who has something you want, ask him how he got it . . . and then go out and do what he did!"

When the old man promised that it was the last time he would make his Sunday speech, he was met by a chorus of insincere voices urging him to reconsider and assuring him that he would live forever. While the sycophantic din was at its apex, Corey asked his Hampa Ham if he might have a few moments alone with him.

His parents and relatives watched Corey and his grandfather sitting out on the veranda. The two seemed to be having a good visit. No one could hear what was being said, but the amount of laughter Corey provoked and the manner in which the two shook hands and embraced was quite disturbing to all the heirs and heiresses.

Hampa Ham passed away the following Sunday.

The reading of the will was held in the library of the Holly Hills mansion. Most of Charles Hammersberg's blood relatives were openly angry at what they learned. One nephew's face turned beet-red as he sounded off at the grievous injustice he had been done by that "selfish old bastard who bored us to shit every Sunday preaching that damned sermon."

Cynthia Carter was saddened by her father's death, but quite pleased at her son's extreme good fortune. She did wonder why her father had chosen to award Corey ten million dollars when she was bequeathed but five million and her husband only a hundred thousand and an old Packard touring car. In the quiet of their bedroom, Paul insisted that it was they who were responsible for their son's windfall inheritance. It was they who had taught him his good manners and courteous behavior. Cynthia suggested that perhaps Corey himself had played a part in winning the huge inheritance. She reminded Paul of how their son had utterly endeared himself to her father when he had mangled the pronunciation of his name.

"Nobody in the history of the universe ever gave a

person ten million dollars for accidentally inventing a silly nickname like Hampa Ham," Paul argued. "It was the upbringing that did it!"

In fact, it was neither the painstaking parenting nor the cute baby talk that had tilted the scales in Corey's favor. It was the admissions he had made to his grandfather on that fateful last Sunday. He had admitted to his Hampa Ham how, when he was young, he had dreaded coming to the Sunday dinners knowing that he would have to suffer through a boring lecture before getting his cake and ice cream. He told how, to keep his sanity, he started to time the speech and try to guess its length. He told too how he had memorized "The Hammersberg Address" and had amused himself by learning to say it backward. He demonstrated his ability to do this and was surprised when his grandfather laughed and asked that he do it again.

Corey then admitted that the speech had absolutely no meaning to him "until today."

"When I heard you speak today," Corey said, "I felt that you were talking to me. I'm eighteen now and I know what I want to do with my life. I want to be like you, Hampa Ham, a multi-multimillionaire. In your speech you say, 'Timidity will get you nowhere!' . . . And 'You live in the dark if you don't ask questions,' and 'If there is someone who has what you want, ask them how they got it and go do what they did.' Well, Hampa Ham, I'm asking. How did you get to be a multi-multimillionaire?"

The old man, rasping and wheezing, told of a man whom he had much admired.

"My uncle Zeke, smart man . . . went to South America, discovered a tin mine, and became rich manufacturing cans. When I turned seventeen he asked me what I wanted for my birthday and I told him, 'I want to be rich like you.' I asked him to give me a hundred thousand dollars and he did. I invested it in a lot of things, Coca-Cola, blue-chip stocks, long-term federal bonds. I made a fortune."

Corey, inspired by the story, explained that a hundred thousand dollars then was more like a million today and asked if he could have a million dollars. The old man shook his head and said that he was pleased that his grandson had learned something from the lecture and requested Corey say it backward "one more time."

When Corey finished, the old man laughed, kissed his grandson on the cheek, and informed him that his arithmetic was wrong.

"Son, a hundred thousand back then was more like ten million today."

So Corey asked for ten million . . .

Lance and Gwendolyn
A Modern Fairy Tale

LANCE BENSEN pushed the button for the twentieth floor then quickly pressed the door-open button when he saw her coming down the hall. His heart stopped and his eyelids locked open as he stared at the apparition coming toward the elevator.

"Guinevere," he muttered, looking at the real-life embodiment of an illustration of Lady Guinevere that adorned the cover of his copy of *Lancelot and Guinevere*. Lady Guinevere, the willowy figure to whom, twenty years ago on his thirteenth birthday, he had secretly plighted his troth. The long, filmy gown Lady Guinevere wore allowed him only a hint of her dainty sandaled feet. He had fantasized so many times that her legs would look exactly like the long, perfectly sculptured ones that now made their way toward him. She glided into the elevator, smiled, and whispered a "Thank you" so deeply sensual that he started to perspire.

"What floor, please?" he asked, praying it would be the highest.

"Eighty-one, please."

"Incredible!" he blurted out.

"I beg your pardon?"

"Uh, incredible," he stammered, pushing the button, "that man has been able to build something eighty-one stories high."

She smiled and nodded. He checked the floor indicator and saw that he had less than seventy floors in which to confess his undying love for her.

"Hello, my name is Lance Bensen. I'm an attorney at Bensen, Harris, and Reissman. Our offices are on the twentieth floor. You may think me mad but I assure you I am a sane and responsible person. A moment ago, when you approached the elevator, my heart stopped. Do you believe in love at first sight?"

"Well, frankly," she said cautiously, examining his face, "I never thought I did."

"But you do now?"

She smiled mysteriously and nodded. He could not believe that she hadn't slapped his face, much less answered his question the way she had.

"On my eleventh birthday," Lance explained rapidly, "my father gave me an illustrated edition of *Lancelot and Guinevere* and I fell in love with the illustration of Lady Guinevere. To this day I am haunted by that image. Am I frightening you?"

"On the contrary," she answered excitedly. "I know the book you're describing. It's a black book with a colored inset of them on the cover."

"Yes, yes, by Lawrence Dempsey," he continued, his enthusiasm mounting, "and there is an illustration of Guinevere and Lancelot at the beginning—"

"Of the third chapter! I have that book! What an amazing coincidence. What did you say your name was?"

"Lance, Lance Bensen . . ."

"Lance? No!" she said, laughing.

"My mother gave me the book," he answered, glancing at the indicator and noting that he had but a few floors to win the hand of the fair maiden.

"This may sound infantile, but I have judged every girl I've ever met against the image of this glorious woman. I can admit it now, but it may be the reason I'm not married. I've been waiting for her. You think I'm crazy, don't you?"

She smiled at him with a warmth and understanding that sent a rush of blood through his entire body.

"Sir, I am probably one of the few people who wouldn't think you crazy. In fact, I can't believe you are saying all this to me."

"You're not angry?"

"How could I be angry at a kindred spirit?" she asked.

She had called him a kindred spirit! He could barely keep himself from grabbing her hand and pressing it to his lips.

"That magical illustration," she continued, "had the same profound effect on me. I too was forever looking for a man who resembled Sir Lancelot. I knew it was silly and childish but . . ."

The elevator slowed, and he knew he must say something that would keep this encounter from being a brief one. The doors opened and before he could think of what to say, she stepped off the elevator, turned to him, and smiled.

"Do you have a moment?" she asked hopefully.

A moment? he thought. How about an eternity?

"Yes," he said, attempting to sound casual. "Um, my first meeting isn't for half an hour."

"Well, then," Lady Guinevere said, beckoning him with her finger, "follow me."

"To the ends of the earth," he muttered to himself.

He followed her down the hall, lagging back far enough to enjoy the graceful sway of her hips. She stopped at an office door where gold letters in script informed him that the name of his fantasy woman was Gwendolyn Lord.

She opened the door and, with what he perceived as a devilish smile, bade him enter. She glided to her desk, picked up a large silver frame, and handed it to him.

"Guinevere and Lancelot, from the book," he said, shaking his head in disbelief. "You had it framed!"

Gwendolyn picked up another frame from her desk and gave it to him. It seemed to be an exact duplicate of the illustrated page.

"You framed two of these?"

"Look at them closely," she said.

"I am. This one is a photograph of the illustration."

"You're very kind, but that's me and my husband, Marvin. It's our wedding picture, taken three weeks ago. Doesn't Marvin look exactly like the Sir Lancelot in the illustration?"

Reluctantly, he admitted that Marvin was the spitting image of the handsome knight. Lance congratulated her on her marriage, bade her farewell, and walked sadly out of her office and out of her life.

Though Lance and Gwendolyn worked in the same building, they did not see each other until two years later, when Gwendolyn asked Lance if he would handle her divorce.

"My husband, Marvin," she explained, "is the very embodiment of what Sir Lancelot was really like. A medieval, womanizing, male-chauvinist schmuck."

Lance and Gwendolyn were married a year and a half later and are considered by all, themselves included, to be a relatively happy couple.

G. G. Giggler

"KIRK, WHY in heaven's name did you bring that girl here?"

"Don't you remember, sis? You wanted to keep your boy-girl seating arrangement intact and suggested I bring a date."

"I meant an appropriate date. You couldn't consider this Gigi an appropriate date."

"Not Gigi. G.G. She uses her initials."

"Does Miss Initials have a name?"

"Ginny Giggler."

"Well, her name's appropriate. Kirk, does she ever stop giggling?"

"I hope not. I enjoy her giggle, it's melodic."

"It's annoying."

"G.G. is a happy person."

"Or blissfully ignorant."

"Sis, you always find happy people annoying. You should look into that."

"What's she so happy about, her height?"

"And her hair, teeth, and legs. Did you notice that she has an astounding figure?"

"I noticed how parts of her astounding figure jiggle when she giggles. Kirk, you've got to get that Amazon out of here before Dad arrives."

"I can't do that. I promised G.G. that she'd finally get to meet Dad."

"What do you mean, 'finally get to meet Dad'? How long have you known the Giggler?"

"About two months, but I didn't really get to know what an extraordinary person she is until she moved in with me."

"Are you serious?"

"Deadly. I've asked her to marry me."

"No!"

"We've set the time and place. Atlantic City, the day after the Miss America pageant if she loses. If she wins, we'll marry a year later, the day she finishes her reign. Save the dates, sis, September eighteenth, either 1999 or the year 2000."

"Kirk, please tell me that this is one of your practical jokes!"

"No joke, sis. I'm so in love with this girl that I hope she loses. I say that knowing how much she wants to wear that crown."

Prissy was hoping to see her brother's face break into the silly Cheshire cat smile that inevitably preceded a "Just kidding, sis!" No smile broke. He's telling the truth, she thought. That bastard is going to change the whole raison d'être of my dinner party. My "Welcome-Back-from-the-Dead-Daddy!" celebration will become a "Welcome-to-the-Family-G.G.!" disaster. Instead of discussing Daddy's remarkable recovery from his heart attack, they'd be hearing all about Miss Giggler's dreams of becoming this year's Miss Friggin' America!

Prissy's hopes for salvaging her party were dealt a blow when she heard the front door open and her father's voice ask, "And who might you be, little lady?" Two short giggles bracketed her response, "I'm G.G., Kirk's friend." Her father saying, "Well, aren't we pretty," was Prissy's cue to hurry to him and stop any further bonding with the bimbo. Prissy was slowed by the clusters of guests who insisted on telling her how beautiful she looked and how grateful they were to be at her party. Prissy had invited an equal mix of honest and dishonest gushers, all of whom owed Kirk Kingsley Senior either money, homage, or their livelihood.

"Prissy, my dear," Kirk Senior sang, greeting his daughter with a peck on the cheek, "what do you think of our Miss Giggler here?"

"*Our* Miss Giggler, Dad?" Prissy asked pointedly. "What do you mean, *our* Miss Giggler?"

"It's all right, darling, I know all about it. Your brother called me last night and spilled the beans."

"What beans are those?"

"Prissy, dear, I know you planned for this to be a surprise party, but your brother worried that my heart got all the shocks it could take from those damned defibrillator paddles. Prissy," he declared, putting his arm around G.G.'s waist, "I want to thank you for arranging this engagement party for your brother and his fiancée. Did you know that this lovely future sister-in-law of yours is going to be in the Miss America pageant?"

"Yes, and isn't it wonderful!" Prissy lied, taking G.G.'s hand. "And I think she's going to win. I can't imagine anyone at the pageant being more beautiful, can you, Kirk?"

"Well, no," her brother said, smiling and moving to his fiancée, "but beauty is not the only thing the contestants are judged on. Talent and intelligence are at least as important, and believe me, G.G. is no slouch in either of those departments."

Hearing G.G giggle too long and too loudly at her brother's nonhumorous pronouncement made Prissy realize what she had to do: Expose her future sister-in-law by making her the focus of attention for the evening. It would keep her company entertained and might stop her brother from destroying his life. She would become Larry King and Miss Giggler would be her sole guest. The one-on-one interview started as they sat down to dinner.

"Sooooo, Gigi, dear," Prissy began, unfolding her napkin. "Tell us about yourself. Where are you from?"

"Well," G.G. giggled, "it's a really funny story and most people laugh when I tell them."

"Oh, tell us, dear," Prissy prompted. "We can all use a good laugh."

"Well, I was born in Walla Walla," she giggled, "where those sweet onions are grown? Now, this may sound like I'm making it up, but when I was six," she continued, failing to suppress a series of high-pitched giggles, "my father, who works for the Coca-Cola company, was transferred from Walla Walla to Maui, where they grow even sweeter onions. Can you believe that?"

The dinner guests managed forced smiles, but Prissy was unhappy to note that her father was beaming from ear to ear.

"So how was it living in the Hawaiian Islands?" Prissy asked, feigning interest. "Was it fun?"

"Well," G.G. said, starting a new series of giggles, "as my mother always says, 'We didn't stay there long enough to get a tan.' Daddy was called back to Atlanta and assigned to . . . now, where do you think?" She stopped giggling long enough to say, "Vidalia, Georgia, where they grow the sweetest onions of all!"

"Well, isn't that interesting," Prissy gushed.

"It gets even more interesting," G.G. giggled.

"I don't see how it can. Tell us," Prissy prodded.

"Well, while we were living in Georgia," G.G. giggled demurely, "I entered my very first beauty contest and I won. Guess what I was crowned?"

"Miss Onion?" Prissy asked amiably.

"No," she giggled, "Miss *Sweet* Onion, but you were

close. Kirk!" she whooped. "You told your sister about me being Miss Sweet Onion, didn't you?"

"I did not, honey."

"Oh, Kirky, you're joshing." G.G. giggled, turning to Prissy. "Your brother told you, didn't he?"

"No, he didn't," Prissy said sweetly, kissing her pinkie to God, "I swear!"

"If that is so," G.G. cooed, sniffing the air, "then who is responsible for the smell I'm smelling?"

Embarrassed laughter erupted from everyone but an elderly banker who had passed wind moments earlier and was sure he had gotten away with it.

"G.G., darling," Kirk remarked, "that wasn't a very diplomatic way of—"

"Of saying that I smelled French onion soup?" she asked innocently. "That is on your menu, isn't it, Prissy?"

"How did you know?" Prissy asked. "The kitchen door is closed. Does anyone else smell the soup?"

All shook their heads.

"Another one of G.G.'s talents that I didn't know she had," Kirk said, proudly patting her shoulder.

"You ought to add it to your talent résumé," Prissy offered as the butler entered carrying a silver tureen. "Those extra points might be the margin of victory."

"It is so amazing," giggled G.G., ignoring Prissy's sarcasm, "that you would be serving me onion soup when I was telling you how onions have been such a big part of my life. Prissy, I am so happy you made this soup. It'll make my onion story that much more interesting when I tell it again."

A contented Prissy smiled sweetly as she listened to G.G. giggling and rattling on about onions and onion soup. Ginny Giggler was having the desired negative effect on the guests and, more important, on Kirk Senior. During the soup course, she decided to go in for the kill.

"You know, G.G., I have seen every Miss America pageant in the last ten years," Prissy offered, "and do you know what I've observed?"

"Prissy, I do want to know," G.G. said, putting her spoon down, "but before you tell me I have to say a word about this onion soup. I swear, it is the best I have ever eaten. Now, if you don't want to give out your culinary secrets, I'd understand, but if you do, I'd love to have your recipe for this."

"And you shall have it," Prissy said sweetly. "I'll write it out for you."

"Oh, thank you. Now when I tell my onion story," she giggled, "I can add that Prissy Kingsley gave me the recipe for the world's most delicious French onion soup."

Prissy was thrilled with the reception G.G.'s stories were getting. All of her guests' eyebrows were raised, and the few who weren't eating had their mouths open. Kirk was aware of what his sister was doing, but had faith that by evening's end everyone would love and respect G.G. as he did.

"Prissy," G.G. said, remembering, "you said that you observed something about the pageant?"

"Oh, yes," Prissy recalled happily. "I noticed in the last few years that the girls who won were not always the prettiest but were the ones who gave the best and the most sincere answers to the master of ceremonies' questions."

"Yes, it's true," G.G. agreed innocently.

"Well," Prissy continued, "I wondered if you've given much thought to how you might answer those questions."

"Oh, I have," she giggled. "We're not told what the questions will be, but that's the challenge. I think I'll be ready for whatever they ask. You know what might be fun," she said, giggling a short giggle. "I hope I'm not monopolizing your dinner . . . I have been going on a bit, haven't I?"

A chorus of sarcastic "Oh nos" and "Not at alls" and "Don't be sillys" were misread by G.G. and gave her leave to suggest that it might be fun if she answer questions that Prissy or any of her guests cared to ask.

"It would be so helpful," G.G. pleaded. "Would you mind?"

"Not at all," Prissy offered willingly. "If you become Miss America, we can all say we helped. Are you ready?"

"Yes, I am!"

"G.G., darling," Kirk interjected angrily, "do you think this is a good idea?"

"Oh, I do," G.G. insisted. "Fire away, Prissy!"

"Miss Sweet Onion, if you—"

"Miss Georgia!" G.G. corrected gently.

"Sorry! Uh, Miss Georgia, if you were to become Miss America, how would you use your power to improve mankind?"

G.G. sat up straight in her chair, squared her shoulders, and took a deep breath. She was the only one in the room who seemed unaware that these posture adjustments called attention to her perfectly proportioned bosom. Poised and confident, G.G. closed her eyes and took the time she needed to formulate her answer. Whatever it was, Prissy expected it to contain many inanities and much giggling.

"If I were to become Miss America," G.G. said in a well-modulated contralto voice, "I would do everything in my power to save human lives, be it as a doctor of medicine or as a lawmaker. If, in my lifetime, I am able to save one life, I will consider it a life well spent."

No one at the table seemed to care that she was speaking drivel. They had expected as much, but no one had imagined that she could say whole sentences without giggling. That surprised even her fiancé, who had never before heard her speak in this low, mellow voice. Kirk Senior was quite aware of the nasty little game his daughter was playing. Prissy's displeasure with her brother's choice of mate was apparent and understandable, but he was not about to take sides. G.G.'s shortcomings were apparent, but so too was her beauty. He popped a piece of warm sourdough bread into his mouth and thought seriously about using Miss Georgia as a spokesperson for Pleasure, the international cosmetics firm he had recently acquired.

Disappointed that her pigeon was able to suppress her giggle, Prissy gambled that Miss Sweet Onion could not suppress her stupidity.

"Tell us, Miss Georgia," Prissy asked. "When you say your goal is to save lives as a doctor or as a lawmaker, what exactly did you mean by lawmaker?"

"Well, I'd like to be a United States senator," G.G. stated simply, "and help to draft legislation that outlaws things that takes people's lives."

"Such things as?"

"Nuclear weapons, wars, guns, land mines, pollution, poverty, electric chairs, lethal injections ... things like that."

Most of the guests were able to stifle their laughter, and encouraged by this and her father's reaction, Prissy pressed on.

"Miss Georgia, when you said 'save lives as a doctor' are we to assume that you intend to study medicine?"

"I intend to *continue* studying medicine, and hopefully by next semester I will have my degree in endocrinology. However, I won't decide which career I'll pursue until after I earn my master's in political science, which may take a year or more unless," G.G. added, smiling warmly,

"I cut down on my volunteer work at the AIDS clinic and the senior citizens' hospices, which I would not like to do."

As she was asking it, Prissy wondered whether she would regret quipping, "When the hell do you go to the toilet?"

This flippancy gave everyone who had been stifling laughter permission to explode, and explode they did. Prissy was stunned by the reaction and proud that she had succeeded in ridiculing her brother's fiancée while amusing her dinner guests. Some were laughing so heartily that she considered topping herself with, "Or have you decided to hold it in until after you're elected senator?"

One of the guests, who had a silly, high-pitched cackle, became the catalyst for the more repressed laughers to become convulsed. Feeding off the cackler and each other, many were soon holding their sides, wiping tears from their eyes and asking each other to "Stop, stop, stop." Two men were laughing soundlessly, with their arms thrashing about and their mouths wide open. G.G., who had every right to feel mortified and angry, was deathly calm and stared straight ahead. Kirk tried to put his arm around his fiancée, but she pushed his arm aside defiantly and shouted, "Get out of my way, Kirk!," then strode toward the door. An apologetic Kirk followed closely behind G.G. and almost knocked her over when she stopped short at the head of the table. Kirk's father was one of the men G.G. saw flailing his arms and laughing soundlessly. He was trying to tell somebody that he couldn't breathe. Only G.G. recognized that he had something lodged in his esophagus. The laughter cut off abruptly when G.G. shouted to everyone, "Shut up!"

"Mr. Kingsley is choking," G.G. announced, standing behind the gasping man. "Is there a doctor in the house?"

"I invited his doctor, but he couldn't make it," a devastated and guilt-ridden Prissy explained as she raced to her father. "Aren't you a doctor, G.G.?"

"He needs a Heimlich maneuver, which I can do, but with his heart condition, I would have liked . . ."

Without waiting for an opinion or permission or physical help from either of his children, G.G. lifted the 190-pound tycoon out of his chair, placed her fist under his rib cage, and deftly applied the Heimlich maneuver. He coughed up a small piece of sourdough bread and managed a sickly smile before fainting. G.G. correctly diagnosed him as being oxygen-deficient and ordered Kirk to fetch the oxygen canister that she assumed would be in his bedroom.

On September 18, 1999, Kirk J. Kingsley and all the business and blood members of his family drove in a motorcade of stretch limousines to Atlantic City's convention hall where they rooted noisily for Miss Georgia to win the big prize.

After watching G. G. Giggler graciously acknowledge the thunderous applause and the standing ovation she received for her flawless piano rendition of Gershwin's Concerto in F, a happy but conflicted Kirk convinced himself that there were worse things in life than having to wait a year before marrying the last Miss America of this century.

Deibenquist Sounds Famous

"So, Scoop, darling, what do you think?"

"I like it, Ceil. I really do. It's easy on the eyes and it's modern, just like you described it. It's a very pleasant painting, very pleasant."

"Isn't it? I think it would fit in perfectly with the color scheme I'm planning for the dining room."

"And the price isn't out of line, considering what they're getting for paintings these days."

"Whorley Deibenquist. Is he very famous?"

"Well, I don't know about *very* famous but he must be famous enough. No one asks thirty thousand dollars for a painting unless they're some kind of famous. You know, I think I've heard of him. Whorley Deibenquist! He *sounds* famous."

"Like Pablo Picasso?"

"Nobody is as famous as Picasso, hon. Pablo got fifty-four mill for one of his jobs. No, this Deibenquist isn't in the same league with ol' Pablo."

"How do we know he's any good?"

"The price, Ceil. The price tells you how good anyone is. Would they give Evander Holyfield thirty million dollars for a fight if he wasn't good?"

"He wasn't very good at his last fight."

"Good enough so that no one asked him to give the money back."

"If this artist is so good, why is the painting only thirty thousand?"

"That's because he's young. I'll bet when Picasso was this guy's age he wasn't getting thirty thou a painting. He was lucky to get thirty pesos. I say we buy it."

"Really?"

"Of course really. Isn't that why you had me look at it?"

"You're right, but maybe you can offer him eighteen thousand, tell him I'm a decorator."

"But you're not."

"I have my cousin's resale number."

"Ceil, you don't bargain for great art."

"How do we know it's great art?"

"Well, for one thing, he painted the trees so they don't look exactly like trees but we can tell they are."

"That's true. Scoop, how about that painting we saw at Sheila's friend's studio? The sky had a very similar soft pink color that I want to use for the walls. It was much larger than this one and she wanted only eight hundred dollars for it."

"Honey, we got a custom-built home. Do you want to

cock it up with a eight-hundred-dollar piece of art that was painted by your cousin Sheila's girlfriend what's-her-name?"

"You're right, darling. We don't even know her name. Oh, I hope this one fits in with my decor. I'm only guessing that the colors will match."

"You got a good eye, Ceil. You found those great tangerine throw pillows that match the walls in my waiting room. I don't know how you did that."

"Well, I did cheat a little, Scoop. I took a tangerine with me when I went looking for those pillows. I wish I had brought a paint sample with me. I don't know, darling, I am so undecided about this Deibenquest painting."

"Deiben*quist*."

"What?"

"You said Deiben*quest*. It's Deiben*quist*."

"Well, I wish Mr. Deiben*quist* had painted in some more birds in flight. I wonder if he would."

"I don't think so, honey. The painting is called '*Bird* in Flight.'"

"He could change it to '*Birds* in Flight.' That's easy enough to do."

"I know, pumpkin, but you can't ask an artist to paint in extra birds if he don't feel they belong."

"But the bird is the perfect powder blue I need. It would help so much if it were a bigger bird. Could we ask him to make the bird bigger?"

"No, artists don't work that way."

"Suppose you tell him that he has a definite sale if he adds a couple of more birds?"

"Ceil, with a real artist it's a take-it-or-leave-it proposition, that much I know."

"You're probably right. I like the painting. I know it won't clash with our floral dinnerware and the color of the bird is a perfect match for the seat cushions. I just wish that bird were a little bigger . . ."

"I trust your eye, Ceil. Here's how I look at it. The colors aren't a perfect match, but if you can live with the painting for a year, I'll put it up for auction. If the gallery owner wasn't handing me a load of bull manure about this Deibenquist guy, my guesstimate is that we'll end up with a couple of thou profit."

Editor's note: Both Ceil and Scoop guessed wrong. The colors were way off. (The sky was many shades lighter than Ceil's walls and the small blue bird did not match her seat cushions.) Ceil suffered with her mistake for a year before insisting that Scoop sell "the damned thing." Scoop's guesstimate of a couple of thousand dollars' profit was even further off. It was auctioned at Sotheby's for 900,000 dollars, giving him an 870,000-dollar profit. Ceil used 800 of it to buy a seascape from Sheila's friend, who, for an extra hundred, painted in a flock of blue seagulls.

How Paul Robeson Saved My Life

I WAS AWARE that the master sergeant who was urinating beside me was a Negro, and I tried to behave as if it was the most natural thing in the world. It wasn't. It was 1943, and the United States Army was just starting to consider treating all men equally. The only integrated barracks at Camp Crowder, Missouri, was this one that housed a training school for noncommissioned officers. Being a corporal, I barely qualified as a noncommissioned officer. I wanted so badly for this black man to know how pleased I was that we were in an integrated latrine standing shoulder to shoulder and pissing for our country! A few moments later, once again side by side, we washed our hands. I ventured a "Hi" and got a "Hi" back. We started a conversation that began with "What outfit are you with?" and ended five minutes later with our having mutual knowledge of each other's hometowns, schooling, marital status, and favorite jazz singers.

I was aware that at the far end of the latrine a blond, crew-cut tech sergeant stood urinating and observing us engaging in social intercourse. He kept glaring at me as he buttoned his fly. I thought we must have really upset him, because why would he leave without washing his hands?

The master sergeant and I shook hands and wished each other luck surviving the war. He climbed to the second floor of the barracks where the "colored" noncoms were assigned and I went to my bunk on the ground floor where I found the blond, crew-cut sergeant sitting on my footlocker.

"Staff Sergeant Andrew 'Bull' Warrington," he said, extending his unwashed hand.

"Corporal Carl Reiner," I shot back, reluctantly taking his hand.

I gave him a wet fish handshake instead of my normal manly one and immediately regretted it, for I had now advertised myself as a Jewish sissy while still risking an infection. I started to ask him where he hailed from, but he interrupted me to ask if I didn't think it was a "fuckin' shame" that we had to live with "the damn niggers." My hesitation was all the answer he needed.

"Corporal," he said, squinting at me, "are you sayin' you don't mind livin' with niggers?"

"They're not really living *with* us," I explained, "they're living *above* us."

I wondered if the sergeant noticed that I referred to our black brethren as "they" instead of "niggers." I was considering saying Negroes, which was the choice of most of us nonracists back then, but I chickened out. Visions of the Ku Klux Klan were dancing in my head.

"It don't bother you, Corporal, that they're puttin' their black asses on our toilet seats and usin' our fuckin' showers? That don't bother you damn Yankees, does it?"

Being born of Austro-Romanian parents, I had never thought of myself as a damn Yankee. I was flattered. I told the sergeant as politely as I could that it didn't bother me that we were sharing the latrine, unless they pissed on the toilet seats or shat in the shower.

"I'd be annoyed," I added, "if anyone did that, present company included."

A few of the noncoms chuckled, and I suspected that among them I had an ally or two.

"Are you sayin' that you think a fuckin' nigger is as good as a white man?" Sergeant Warrington asked bluntly.

We were now back in the eleventh century, he, the inquisitor, and I, the heretic, but how to tell His Holiness that he was full of shit without putting myself in danger of being lynched?

"You ask," I said, enunciating each word slowly, with a quasi-Shakespearean delivery, "if I consider that a fucking nigger is as good as a white man?" I rubbed my chin thoughtfully and said, "I honestly don't know. That Sergeant Williams seemed like a pretty nice guy."

"You tellin' me," he exploded, "that that fuckin' nigger is as good as you?!"

"Probably better," I suggested. "I know he's a lot better educated than I am, and in hand-to-hand combat I bet he can beat the shit out of both of us."

I worried that I had gone too far, but a few noncoms laughed out loud and I relaxed. I had found my strategy. Laughs! I'll go for laughs!

When I heard the snap in his voice, I knew the battle was joined.

"You sayin', Corporal, that a nigger could be as good as a white man?"

"I am saying, Sergeant, that it is within the realm of possibility that a *particular* nigger could, in some ways, be as good as or even superior to a *particular* white man."

"And I'm telling you, Corporal," the sergeant explained as if I were a schoolchild who had missed a lesson, "there is no fuckin' nigger in this world as good as me, and there is sure as shit no fuckin' black-assed coon *superior* to me."

"Somewhere in this vast world, Sergeant," I dared to suggest, "there might be some niggers who are your equal."

"Name one!" he challenged.

I laughed and told him that we were engaging in a silly exercise. He responded by placing his nose against mine.

"If you can name one," he shouted into my mouth, "I'll kiss your big white ass."

"I accept the challenge, but," I explained, "if by some remote chance I win, I'd rather you kissed someone else's ass. . . . Any volunteers?"

The boys hooted and hollered and some raised their hands.

"CORPORAL," he screamed, "NAME A NIGGER! THAT'S AN ORDER!"

"PAUL ROBESON, SIR!" I answered smartly.

"Paul Robeson. All right, Corporal, you tell me what that nigger has accomplished and I'll match him nine ways to January."

I suggested that we were engaging in a pointless exercise, and he accused me of bluffing and trying to back out of the challenge. When he put his nose up against mine again and insisted I tell him "one fuckin' thing the nigger had done," I informed him that Paul Robeson had graduated Phi Beta Kappa from Rutgers University.

"I never went to college," the sergeant countered proudly, "and never regretted it."

One of the noncoms found this amusing, and I quickly chose him as our scorekeeper.

"Put down one for the sarge and one for Robeson," I instructed. "So far, we're even."

I then offered that Mr. Robeson was fluent in five foreign languages.

"Five *foreign* languages," he said emphatically. "Well, I speak *American!*"

"Two to two," I shouted to my scorekeeper, who laughed and held up two fingers on each hand.

Spurred on by an audience whose responses were heartening, I began to enjoy myself.

The following is a remembered transcript of the historic debate:

Me: Paul Robeson was a four-letter man at his college and was voted an All American in football.

Sarge: I never went to college, and before I enlisted I managed a grocery market. (*chuckles from the group*)

Me: Three to three, still even. Paul Robeson has written a book.

Sarge: This may surprise you, but I never read a book!

Me: It doesn't surprise me. Four to four. Damn! I thought I had you on that one. (*good healthy response from the boys*)

Me: Paul Robeson has a degree in law.

Sarge: My daddy is a lawyer and has an office in downtown New Orleans.

Me: Got me again, damnit. Five to five. Paul Robeson is an actor and a singer and has appeared on Broadway, in concert, and in motion pictures.

Sarge: And I am (*here he paused for effect*) a Louisiana state board-certified embalmer and I have worked as a chief embalmer in the biggest mortuary in Shreveport.

On hearing this, I threw my hands up and conceded defeat. I congratulated him on the brilliance of his strategy, playing possum, and waiting for just the right moment to drop the bomb. I admitted that if Paul Robeson were called upon to embalm a finger, much less a whole corpse, he would be at a loss. I then patted the sergeant on the back, grinned, and good-naturedly called him a sonofabitch for booby-trapping me the way he had. He cocked his head and wondered if he was being complimented or ridiculed. The sarge concluded from the laughter and chatter that he was being derided. He moved toward me with clenched fists and I fully expected to be punched in the face. Instead, he brushed past me, smiling in that strange way that villains do in westerns when they lose a round to the hero and leave. You know they will return.

That evening, the sarge and I passed each other in the mess hall. I forced a smile and he responded with a sneer that seemed to say "I'm not finished with you!"

At nine o'clock that night, I climbed into my upper bunk and waited for the other shoe to drop. It was lights-out and the barrack was ominously quiet, or so it seemed to me. The soldiers who were not burdened with neurotic guilt and fear were sound asleep before the bugler's last note had faded. And then it came! From across the room, a voice with a gentle southern drawl drifted toward me.

"Corporal Reiner, you awake?"

"Yes, Sergeant?" I whispered back.

"What say you and me step outside with our car-bines?"

"Huh?" was all I could think to say.

"I think, Corporal," he continued sweetly, addressing me as if we were at a cotillion and he was asking me for a dance, "if you and me went into the field with our carbines, we'd find out once and for all which one of us is right about the damn niggers. It'd be fun, don't you think?"

"Yes, Sarge, it could be fun," I said blithely, "but I'm not about to go to jail for life just for a little fun."

I now had the attention of a lot of chuckling witnesses.

"Corporal, what the fuck you talkin' about?"

"I am a first-class marksman," I lied, "with three medals to prove it. If we faced off with carbines, I'd probably blow your head off while your finger was still searching for the trigger. Sarge, I am not going to screw up my life over an argument about racial superiority when you've already won the damned debate."

The men, who had remained noncommittal during the sergeant's invitation to a duel, now erupted with a mélange of laughter, catcalls, a reminder that it was past lights-out, and a suggestion that we "shut the fuck up!"

Within seconds there was a stony silence that I did not expect would last. I knew the sergeant would want the last word, and that word turned out to be my name, Reiner.

"Ryyyyyynuh," he sang, elongating the first syllable to the breaking point, "yyyyew a Jyyyew?"

I admitted I was Jewish and asked why he had asked. With a voice that seemed to brim with nostalgia, he informed me that one of his best friends back home was a "Jyyyew."

"Ben Goldfarb?" he asked expectantly, thinking I would know him because we were both Jewish.

My adrenaline flow had slowed and all I could think to say was, "Ben Goldfarb? No, I don't think I know him."

Those were the last words Sergeant Andrew "Bull" Warrington and I exchanged. About a year later, I learned that the sergeant had been wounded and had received a medical discharge. Some time after that, a non-com who was present at the historic Robeson debate showed me a clipping from the camp paper that told of the sergeant going back to his home in Louisiana and being elected to a seat in the legislature. It did not spell out whether it was a state or a federal seat so I did not know whether to be concerned for the future of his state or the future of our country.

Dear John

June 6, 1999

Dear John,

This is the most difficult letter I have ever written in my life. I seriously considered not writing it, but I remembered what you always told me, "We are nothing if we are not honest."

So, dear John, I am taking your advice and being honest. It hurts me so, but I realize that there is no other way. After much soul-searching, I have decided to call off our wedding.

I know you are saying to yourself, Why did she wait till three days before the ceremony to do this? John, when I explain, you'll realize that you are partly to blame. Last week after dinner

at Mercurio's, which, by the way, was delicious——and I know how expensive it was even
though my menu didn't have the prices on it. I
know what real caviar costs and I really dug in,
didn't I? Well, that night, as always, you were
too generous, and it is because of your generosity
that I'm calling off our relationship.

I don't know how many times you have said
to me that everything you have is mine. I always
believed you meant it, but I don't know if you
ever believed that I believed you. When you said
that after we were married, I'd be an equal partner in your dry-cleaning store, I believed you.
But, that night at the restaurant, you went too
far. I was only joking when you were paying the
bill and I said, "Is your wallet mine too?," and
to prove your point, you insisted I take it and
keep it. Well, as you know, I didn't keep it but
sent it right back in that insured package. John,
you should never have let me take that wallet
home. You see, I looked through it and found

this picture of you and your uncle Dominic, the one at the beach in Maui in front of a hotel. You did tell me about him, but you never mentioned what an extremely attractive man he is.

I showed the picture to my mother, and she noticed that on the back he had written "Dominic Saltero at sixty-three and my nephew John at thirty-nine." Mom and I both agreed that he was the best-looking sixty-three-year-old we'd ever seen. Mom insisted I give him a call to invite him to our wedding, and I did. He was very nice and said that you had sent him a snapshot of me. He told me I was very pretty, and I told him what a generous man you are, and how I got to see his picture because you had given me your wallet. I must say, John, you and your uncle Dominic are so much alike.

He said that if I could get out of my commitment to you, everything he had would be mine, including the hotel he owns that you two were standing in front of. Yesterday, Dominic wired money for airfare, and Mom and I are at the airport now. We leave for Hawaii in ten minutes, so I don't have time to write more. I'll send you a card when I get there.

I hope you're not too angry with me, but you did say that anything you had was mine, and that I could have whatever I want. Well, I want your uncle Dominic. Thank you, and God bless you, John . . . I know he will.

Sincerely yours,

Mary

P.S. You won't find anything missing from your wallet except the stamp I used for this letter, and now you have that back too.

Sissy Sue and the Reverend Reverend

SISSY SUE MERKER boarded the bus, made her way down the aisle, and chose a seat that was not above a wheel.

"Is this taken?" she asked the birdlike woman who was settling into the window seat.

The woman shook her head.

"Well, then, if you don't mind, I'll take it," Sissy Sue said as she sat on the woman's pocketbook. "Oh, look what I did!" she cried, retrieving the soft leather purse and handing it to the woman. "I don't know why I didn't see it sitting there. I feel so stupid. Did I crush anything?"

"Just my glasses," the woman said, retrieving the bent frames, "but they were cheap ones."

"That is just like me," Sissy Sue said, opening her purse. "How much were they?"

"I don't know, I bought them at the drugstore. I think six dollars."

"Well, here's six dollars," Sissy Sue said, digging the bills out of her wallet. "I've been doing stupid things all my life, the least I can do is pay for them. Each year I seem to be getting a tad stupider. God knows I have tried to reverse the process, but with no success, that is, until . . ." Sissy smiled and looked at the woman beseechingly. "May I tell you a little story? Well, last week," Sissy Sue proceeded without waiting for an answer, "I enrolled at the Center for Self-Improvement for a six-week course called 'Overcoming Your Stupidity' . . . and guess what? I sent in a check for two hundred dollars and I forgot to sign it. Now, if that isn't stupid. By the time I sent a signed check, the class was full up. It's a comfort to know that there are so many people who know they're stupid and want to do something about it."

Sissy Sue took a deep breath, faced the woman, and smiled triumphantly.

"Do you know why I'm smiling?" Sissy Sue asked.

The woman shook her head.

"I'm going to ask for my money back. I don't think I'll be needing that course because, last Wednesday, fate stepped in and took my hand. I was in the produce department of the Piggly Wiggly market where I got to chatting with this nice woman, and I was telling her my problem just as I'm telling you, and she told me about this evangelical minister in Greenville, South Carolina, whom she saw work miracles. With her own eyes she saw this minister make a lame girl walk, a blind man see, and a diabetic woman throw her pills away. Well, I told her that I've seen those kinds of miracles on TV many times. She had too, but then she went on to describe this one case where the reverend got a retarded man to recite 'Casey at the Bat,' and Joyce Kilmer's 'Trees,' and the whole 'To Be or Not to Be' speech from *Hamlet*. Now, I may be stupid, but I was not about to take the word of a perfect stranger who I happened to meet in the market. So, two days ago, I bought a round-trip ticket to Greenville to see the miracle man for myself. This minister, whose name is . . . now you're going to think I'm making this up, but it's Reverend Reverend. That's right, Reverend Reverend. Reverend is his family name and his mama christened him Reverend because she said that when she looked into her baby's eyes, she saw something holy there. The reverend is an ordained minister, and could call himself the Reverend Reverend Reverend, but he just calls himself Reverend Reverend. If I had any doubts about flying all the way to Greenville, they were put to rest as soon as I heard the reverend speak at the Friday night healing session. His voice was real deep, and it had a rumble to it that reminded me of my daddy, only my daddy's voice didn't have the gentleness in it that Reverend Reverend's had in his. I think my daddy's deep voice came from smoking too many cigarettes. Daddy, rest his soul, was tall and heavyset like Reverend Reverend, but the Lord did a better job on proportioning the reverend's body. Would you care for a crystal mint?" Sissy Sue asked, holding up a roll of Life Savers. "Lubricates the throat real nice."

"I will have one," the birdlike lady chirped. "Thank you so much."

"Let me know if you want another," Sissy Sue said, popping a mint into her mouth, "Well, that night, Reverend Reverend announced that he was going to talk about feeling unworthy, and how to change that in ourselves. He asked us to raise our hands if we felt we were unworthy and most of the people did. Naturally, I raised my hand. If you're stupid, you're certainly not worthy. Then the reverend walked up and down the aisle and looked straight into each person's eyes. Lord, that man has beautiful eyes. He asked us why we felt unworthy and everybody told him their reasons. Most people felt unworthy because they had sinned against the Lord. I told him that I was unworthy because I was so damned stupid. He asked me my name and I told him ... I will never forget how sweetly he smiled at me. I swear, his smile is even sweeter than Reverend Falwell's. Well, he took my hand, looked me right in the eye, and said, "Sissy Sue Merker, let's just find out how darned stupid you are. Why don't you stand up and tell us why you think you're so stupid." Ordinarily, I would never stand up in front of all those people and talk about myself, but there was something about Reverend Reverend that gave me the faith to do what he asked. I don't know how long I talked, but I put at least three crystal mints into my mouth. I told about all the stupid things I had done since I was a child. Like when I was four years old, I poured milk from a bottle into a glass that I didn't know was upside down. Mother was angry and called me stupid and I couldn't blame her. We were very poor and I'd wasted all that milk. I told about the time when I was ten and I was helping my mother prepare for Easter dinner and how she had asked me to peel the cooked beets and slice them as soon as they cooled. Just as the guests arrived, I remembered that I hadn't peeled the beets. Now you know how slippery wet, cooked beets can be; well, one squished out of my hand and onto my new white organdy dress. I didn't have another party dress, so my mother made me sit at dinner wearing my school uniform, a green cotton skirt and middy blouse. I don't blame all my cousins for making fun of me. It was my fault for not putting on an apron. The very stupidest thing of all happened at my sweet sixteen birthday party. I told Reverend Reverend that it was too painful for me to talk about even though it was so many years ago. He said those are the things I must share with him if I wanted his help. So, I shared. I told how at my party, Bo Danton asked me if I'd like to sit with him in his daddy's big new car and listen to the radio. 'The Hit Parade' was coming on and he said he wanted to hear if 'Mister Sandman' was still number one. Everyone in school knew about Bo Danton, and why he was called the octopus, but Bo swore he'd behave and wouldn't try any funny stuff. Well, I have living proof that Bo Danton lied to me that night. Billy Bo is now forty-seven years old, and he's the spitting image of Bo. Am I talking too much?" Sissy Sue stopped to ask her rapt traveling companion.

"No, no, it's very interesting." She smiled, adding, "I finished my mint, I chewed it. May I have another?"

"Of course," Sissy Sue replied, tearing open a fresh roll. "I really believed that Bo Danton would sit in a car listening to Snooky Lanson and would not try to get into my panties. I even believed that he would marry me like he said he would when Daddy told him that I was pregnant. He didn't fool Daddy, though. The day Bo left to visit his uncle in Montana, Daddy took me by the hand and marched right into Governor Danton's office, who, at the time, was running for reelection. Daddy told him what his son Bo had done, and unless the governor did the honorable thing, Daddy promised to go to the newspapers and tell them about how Bo had seduced and raped me in the backseat of a state-owned limousine."

Sissy Sue took a deep breath and barreled on. "Now I must say, the governor was an honorable man and gave Daddy a whole lot of money for the baby's upbringing and education, and all he asked is that we leave the state and never come back. Against Mama's wishes, Daddy invested all the money in a lot of little things that he said were real good deals. Most of them weren't, but some made him a lot of money, which he kept reinvesting.

"Before Daddy died last year, he told me I was a very wealthy woman, and unless I did something stupid, Mama and I would have enough money to continue to live in luxury for the rest of our lives and Billy Bo's too. I started to tell Reverend Reverend how badly I felt that Mama had died before she got to use any of the money, but the reverend stopped me and said that he had heard enough and knew he could help me. I could see the sincerity shining out of those steely-gray eyes when he took my face in his two big warm hands and said, 'Thank you, Lord, for sending Sissy Sue Merker to me.' Reverend Reverend spoke to a lot of folks at the prayer meeting, but I was the only one he invited to his office after the meeting. I sat in a big easy chair, and he was so warm and affectionate, in a fatherly way. He took my face in his hands again and this time he put his forehead to mine and prayed silently for a long time, then he kissed me on the forehead and told me again that he would not be able to help me unless I had complete faith in him and told him *everything* about my life. I told the reverend that I had faith in him and that at the meeting I was just going to tell him *the* stupidest thing I had ever done but he had stopped me. I knew it was something he should know about me, and when I told him what I had done, his face became so sad. He shook his head and said, 'Oh, lordy, lordy.' I knew he was disappointed in me but he promised not to abandon me if I put my trust in him. I told him I trusted him although it was hard for me to really trust anyone after my experience with Jan and Timmy Barker. I had trusted them so much that I contributed two million dollars to help them build their

Worship World. Well, I'm sure y'all read about Jan and Timmy and what happened to Worship World. The reverend was very upset and hoped that I had not given 'those charlatans' all the money I had. All but five hundred thousand dollars, I told him. I also told him that I was shocked to hear one man of God call another man of God a charlatan, but he said, 'That's what they were, money-hungry disciples of the devil and the scum of the earth!' He explained how evil impostors like the Barkers made it difficult for the honest and dedicated ministers of the Gospel to do their work. I tell you, the reverend's voice was quivering and his eyes were burning when he gave me his solemn oath to do everything in his power to bring those parasites to justice even if it took every last penny of the money he had worked so many years to save. He was so emotional. I felt awful. I couldn't stand to see this good and decent man in such pain, pain that I was responsible for. So I offered him the little money I had left, but bless him, he said that he had to do this himself. I reminded him that he would really be doing this for me since the Barkers were the ones who had caused me to commit the stupidest act of my life. He said that he could not in good conscience take my last half a million dollars. He was adamant about that and would not be budged until I offered a suggestion. I told him it was probably a stupid idea, but when he heard it, his eyes popped open and his tortured face broke into a smile. 'A loan,' he said, 'of course! Why didn't I think of a loan.

Sissy Sue, you are brilliant.' Those were his exact words, 'Sissy Sue, you are brilliant!' I started to cry and the reverend put his arms around me and promised to repay every penny of the loan and all the money the Barkers had stolen from me just as soon as he won the court case from them."

"As soon as the court case is won," the bird lady repeated. "Is that what he said?"

"His exact words, and look at this," Sissy said to her bemused companion, holding out a five-by-seven colored photo of Reverend Reverend, "he personally autographed it to me. Can you read what it says?"

"To my . . . my . . . I'm sorry," the woman said, squinting at the photo, "I can't make this out without my—"

"Of course, I sat on your glasses," Sissy Sue remembered. "Here, let me read it to you. He wrote, 'To my dear and *worthy* friend, Sissy Sue Merker, God loves you! As does Reverend Reverend Reverend.' And," Sissy Sue added proudly, "see how he underlined *worthy*. The reverend thinks I'm *worthy*. Praise the Lord! I suppose I should stop telling people how stupid I am."

"Yes, you should," sighed her traveling companion. "May I have another crystal mint?"

Creation

HE WONDERED how many before Him had stared at a blank piece of parchment and agonized over what the first word would be.

Where to begin? What to say?

"Start writing," He instructed Himself. "It will come."

He placed his hand on the scroll and was thrilled to see the letter *N* appear. That night, He went to bed happy, knowing that He had done a full and fruitful day's work. The following day was even more productive. He had sat looking at the *N* for less than half a day when an *E* appeared on the parchment, then, miraculously, an *M*, then another *E*, then an *S*, an *I*, and another *S*. He stared at what HIS hand had writ. "NEMESIS," he mouthed. "No, no, this will not do."

With a quick stroke of His sharpened reed, He changed the *N* to a *G* and read aloud, "GEMESIS." His natural writer's instinct told him that what He had writ was good but that a thoughtful rewrite would make it even better. The following morning He awoke at dawn, sprang from His bed, and ran to the scroll. His brain was afire. He reviewed what He had written—GEMISIS. He swiftly replaced the *M* with an *N* and read it aloud slowly, "G-E-N-E-S-I-S."

"Ah, a good beginning," He thought, "a very good beginning."

He read the word out loud many times that day and thought, This could turn out to be a book, a good book.

"Hmmm," He mused, "not *a* good book but *the* good book. Yes," He declared, "THE GOOD BOOK, that is how it shall be known."

He was confident that, with proper handling, *THE GOOD BOOK* would, doubtless, become the biggest best-seller of all time!

That SOB Bastard Eddie

It was lunchtime and Augusta was concerned about her friends Sally and Eddie. It was not like them to be this late for lunch, especially since she had promised them a particularly delicious meal. Sally had developed an annoyingly persistent cough that seemed to be getting worse since winter had come. Augusta had suggested to her friend that if she could not give up cigarettes completely, she should at least try to stop chain-smoking.

"If I stopped chain-smoking, I wouldn't know what to do with my hands," Sally had argued, "and you know what the Bible says about idle hands."

Sally's gentleman friend Eddie was no help. "Smoking is healthy for your lungs," he explained. "The smoke suffocates those germs you breathe in all day."

Eddie and Sally were two impossibly stubborn people. Augusta had given up trying to reform them.

Augusta looked across the plaza at the green pedestal clock in front of the Sherry Netherland Hotel and noted that her friends were inordinately late even for people who had little concept of time. She imagined her friend Sally coughing uncontrollably and collapsing in a gutter somewhere. Augusta looked up at the gray, threatening sky and decided that her friends had opted not to make the long trip uptown because it looked like rain and Eddie hated getting wet.

Augusta had resigned herself to lunching alone when she heard Sally's familiar growly voice complaining about New York's "goddamned crowded subways."

If Augusta had known, she would never have asked about Eddie, because the question triggered a string of curses from Sally that brought on a violent coughing spasm. Augusta patted her friend's back, knowing that it was of little help to someone with emphysema.

Sally's antidote was to chain-light a fresh cigarette. Between coughs she launched into an avalanche of expletives that stopped passersby in their tracks.

"Goddamned-dirty-rotten-sonofabitch-bastard," Sally repeated over and over, "that's what Eddie Reilly is; I'll fix his friggin' wagon."

It was futile to attempt calming her when she was raging about Eddie. Asking what the man had done to her would only fuel her anger, so Augusta waited for the storm to abate before suggesting that they start their lunch without him.

Augusta was particularly proud of her menu that day. She had been able to procure three-day-old tuna fish and avocado sandwiches on whole wheat pita bread and a thirty-two-ounce carton of orange-pineapple juice. She had cadged the juice at The Bagel Shop on Second Avenue by using her favorite gambit. Carrying a large carton of juice that she had picked out of the refrigerator, she would approach a customer who was paying his bill and tell him that she had no money but was "sooo, sooo thirsty" and would appreciate it if he treated her to "this nice, refreshing drink." More often than not the embarrassed or guilt-ridden pigeon would instruct the cashier to add the drink to his bill. The tuna sandwiches were outright gifts from the night manager of the Natural Food Emporium. He remembered Augusta from his old neighborhood. She was his friend Sammy's crazy aunt Gussie, who the kids on the block called "Two-Bit Gussie" because she would toss quarters to them and shout, "Have yourselves a soda on your aunt Gussie."

In those days, Augusta still held down a job as a telephone operator at the Bryant Hotel on Fifty-third Street and Broadway. On weekends, when the horses were not running and she still had carfare, she would travel to Queens and visit with her family.

Augusta had been friends with Sally and Eddie for two years. They met that first winter in a temporary shelter that was hastily organized during a bitter cold spell. Eddie and Sally had endeared themselves to Augusta that first night when she awoke to see them run after and catch a fellow indigent who was making off with her precious rabbit coat. At that moment, a symbiotic trio was born. At night, Sally and Eddie provided security for her and, during the day, Augusta provided food and drink for them.

When Sally calmed down, Augusta signaled that lunch was being served by placing the opened carton of orange-pineapple juice on the concrete bench. Sally immediately grabbed the carton and, between coughs, gulped down huge mouthfuls of the warm juice. Shaking her head, she placed the carton down and started rummaging through the plastic bags burgeoning with her worldly effects. She went through all three of her bags, cursing with frustration as she failed to locate the bottle of red table wine she had hidden the night before.

"That dirty-rotten-sonofabitch-bastard Eddie stole my bottle. I'll fix his wagon!"

"Is this the bottle?" Augusta asked, reaching into the drooping side pocket of Sally's stretched-out cardigan.

Sally snatched the bottle from Augusta, quickly emptied its few remaining drops into the juice carton, and shook it vigorously as she continued to curse Eddie. She explained between sips, coughs, and puffs of her cigarette that she had hidden the bottle from "the sonofabitch bastard," who in the middle of the night had stolen it and guzzled it down.

Augusta tried to lighten the moment by pointing out that Eddie had left enough for her "to make a nice sangria."

Sally would not be mollified, and flung the carton into the street, splattering two well-dressed gentlemen who were headed toward the Plaza Hotel. As they turned to see who had thrown the carton, Sally jumped up and cursed them, their mothers, their wives, their sisters, and their children. Throughout her harangue she interpolated information about Eddie Reilly and what a "sonofabitch bastard" he was and how lucky they were not to be living with "the little weasel."

Augusta made the mistake of grabbing Sally's arm and warning her that if she "didn't stop screaming, somebody would call the police!"

"Screw the police!" Sally shouted. "Screw Eddie and screw you!"

Sally tore open her three bulging plastic shopping bags and continued to curse the police, Eddie, and Augusta, punctuating her invectives by hurling all her sad, soiled blouses and underwear at people who had gathered to watch a bag lady go berserk.

By the time the police arrived, Sally was tearing the clothes off her back and flinging them at the gawkers, some of whom she chased down the street. Augusta had twice tried to restrain Sally, only to be pushed to the ground and kicked. As the police, not too gently, tried to cram a flailing Sally into the back of a police car, she shouted to Augusta, "Gussie, you find that rotten-son-ofabitch-bastard Eddie Reilly and tell him I'm gonna fix his wagon for what he done to me, the dirty-no-good-sonofabitch-bastard!"

As the police car inched its way through the crowd,

Augusta could hear Sally coughing and railing at the "sonofabitch-Eddie Reilly-bastard!"

"Gussie," she exhorted, "go tell that dirty bastard that I'm in jail because of what he done to me!"

Augusta disliked traveling down to the Bowery and walking through the depressing neighborhood. The last time she'd visited her friends there they'd been living in a tin storage shed, behind a recently shuttered hardware store. Augusta knew she had no choice but to search out Eddie and inform him that Sally had been arrested. Augusta collected most of Sally's effects and shoved them back into the begrimed plastic bags.

After a few dozen attempts to pry money out of affluent-looking passersby, she managed to collect enough for the subway ride downtown. Having been there only once, she was surprised by how easily she found the dilapidated hardware store. She made her way up the garbage-strewn alley and squeezed through the opening that Eddie had snipped in the chain-link fence.

Stepping gingerly over old cans and broken bottles, she picked her way to the shed, stopping to watch a large gray rat scurry out of the open door.

"Shoo, rat, shoo!" she shouted, kicking a can at the frightened rat, who made an immediate U-turn and scampered back into the shed. Through the years, Augusta had developed a sensible attitude toward rats.

She understood and accepted their right to forage for food.

"Eddie, it's me, Gussie," Augusta announced, approaching the door. "You know you have rats in your house?"

She threw a soda can against the shed, which sent the rat scurrying out the door and down the alley.

"Eddie, are you in there . . . ?" Augusta called, peering into the unlighted shed.

In the dark, cluttered room, she saw Eddie sitting in a legless club chair. He stared right at her with wide, angry eyes but did not acknowledge her presence.

"Eddie, Sally is mad as hell at you," she informed him. "I don't know what you did to her, but she was telling the world what an SOB you are. The cops arrested her for disturbing the peace. Eddie, besides stealing her wine, what the hell *did* you do to her?"

Eddie continued staring blankly at her and raised no objections when she dug into his shirt pocket and retrieved a respectable-size cigarette butt. She stared back at him and nodded her head knowingly.

"Eddie, you sonofabitch bastard, I know what you did," she sighed as she lit up and blew smoke into his face. "You went and died on her, didn't you?"

Yehudah Benjamin Aronowitz

EVERY NIGHT after work, Yehudah would fix a simple dinner for himself. Tonight it was a boiled potato, two hard-boiled eggs, and a slice of dark bread. Whatever it was, he would eat the meal quickly and rush to his desk. If he didn't write down all the random thoughts that had occurred to him that day, he would consider it a day wasted. This night he wrote:

- HE THAT PAYS THE PIPER, CALLS THE TUNE.
- DEATH CANCELS EVERYTHING BUT TRUTH.
- PREJUDICE IS BEING DOWN ON SOMETHING YOU ARE NOT UP ON.
- NEVER TROUBLE TROUBLE TILL TROUBLE TROUBLES YOU.
- NOTHING IN EXCESS.
- HE WHO EXCUSES HIMSELF, ACCUSES HIMSELF.
- BETTER TO IDLE WELL THAN TO WORK POORLY.
- GO TO LAW FOR A SHEEP AND YOU LOSE YOUR COW.

He added the new page to the immense stack that had been growing for thirty-nine years. Tonight he would bundle up the sheaf of papers and tomorrow he would dispatch it to a publisher. He dipped a newly sharpened quill into the inkwell and on this, his fiftieth birthday, he wrote the letter that, long ago, he had promised himself he would write.

My dear Mr. Bartlett,
      Enclosed please find some thoughts I have jotted down. I hope you will find some of them suitable for publication.

      Very truly yours,

      Yehudah Benjamin Aronowitz

A fortnight later he received the following reply:

Dear Mr. Aronowitz,
      I much enjoyed your "thoughts" and with your permission I would like to include all of them in a new edition that I am readying for publication. As I am sure you are aware, we do not pay a great deal of money for bright sayings, but I daresay that you will derive a measure of satisfaction in seeing your name in a book that includes Shakespeare, Samuel Johnson, La Rochefoucauld, and Aristotle. If you accept our offer, a contract will be sent to you for signature.

      Admiringly,

      Bartlett

Yehudah Benjamin signed the contract, but he regretted initialing the addendum to the contract, which read:

Because we intend to include 150 of your bright sayings in our new Christmas edition we feel strongly that using your full name, Yehudah Benjamin Aronowitz, would hurt sales in the growing anti-Semitic communities. One of our editors suggested we use only your last name, Aronowitz, and shorten it to Aron. I pointed out that Aron suggests Aaron, Old Testament biblical, and I fear it would defeat our purpose. So, we will go forward if you grant us permission to modify your name to Anon. I'm sure you will agree than Anon is both elegant and properly ambiguous.

Warren Waits and the Spaghetti-Strap Girl

WARREN WAITS unlocked his apartment door and considered his options. He could open the door, enter his cozy bachelor apartment, sit down at his desk and pore over a stack of legal briefs, or he could continue standing at the door with his key in the lock and think about returning to the restaurant. Perhaps the maître d' could give him some pertinent information about the magnificent young woman in the black spaghetti-strap dress. Better yet, maybe she was still there.

It had been exactly two years since his wife, Janice, had left him to return to her first husband and her six-year-old daughter. It was small consolation that she'd told him that she would always love him, but could not live one day longer without her "baby." It was only recently that Warren had thought about looking for someone to fill the void in his life Janice had left.

During the twenty-block cab ride home, he had tried to understand how he could have such strong feelings for a woman who had spoken only five words to him. He had been in the process of signing his dinner check when he'd looked up and seen a heavenly vision being seated by the maître d' at a table for four. At the table were an attractive young couple and an empty chair. Warren guessed that they would soon be joined by the "vision's" husband or lover.

When the man arrived, Warren was disappointed to discover that he was not only tall, but handsome. On hearing him being introduced to her as Yuri Gregorivich, he took heart. This, he thought, is a blind date. She is unattached!

If only he hadn't paid his bill, he might have ordered a second cup of coffee and dawdled long enough to learn more about this alluring, short-haired brunette with the beautifully sculpted milk-white shoulders and a liquidy, seductive voice that literally stopped him from inhaling or exhaling. Five words were all she said to him when he retrieved the napkin that had slid off her lap.

Back at his apartment, he recalled the lilt in her voice when she'd said, "Why, thank you, kind sir." It was all the impetus he needed to relock his apartment door, fly down four flights of stairs, and flag a passing cab.

"Bistro d'Amour," Warren shouted. "Two-sixty-seven East—"

"I know where is Bistro," interrupted his Pakistani driver.

"Are you sure?"

"Everybody know Bistro. It's hot new place. Got high marks in *Zagat*."

Warren had no plan for what he was going to do when he returned to the restaurant. He wished he had said more to her than "I believe this is your napkin." Had her blind date not seemed annoyed at the intrusion, he might have said, "I recommend the rack of lamb."

On the return trip to the Bistro d'Amour, Warren fantasized a scenario in which he could get to meet and also impress her.

If a fire broke out in the restaurant and he arrived before the fire department, he would rush in and carry her out of the inferno. She would then look up at him admiringly and say, "Why, thank you, kind sir!"

It could happen, he thought.

He gasped at what he saw when arriving at the Bistro d'Amour. Parked in front was a fire engine, but thankfully no visible fire. There were also three patrol cars, an ambulance, and a large crowd of onlookers standing behind the ubiquitous yellow crime-scene tape. Warren got out of the cab at the blocked-off corner and asked some bystanders what had happened. All agreed that shots had been fired and that there was at least one dead person and maybe one or two wounded.

"Who's dead?" Warren pressed a short, talkative, bald man. "A man or a woman?"

"I'm not sure. I was in there but I ran out. I think it was a man."

"Thank God!" Warren muttered, shocking the bald man.

"But it could've been a female," the man added quickly.

Damn, Warren thought, working his way to the front of the restaurant where he managed to get the attention of a uniformed officer.

"Officer, my name is Warren, uh, John Warren," he said politely, withholding his real name, "and I dined at the restaurant tonight."

"Were you one of those who ran out?" the officer asked casually.

"No, I walked out, but I did dine there. I had the rack of lamb—"

"Were you there when the shots were fired?"

"No, but I can identify some of the diners . . . ones who might have been hit!"

"Who're you talking about?" the officer asked, taking out a pad.

"Uh, well, two young couples who were sitting in a corner of the dining room."

"Can you describe them?"

"Oh, yes. I spoke with one of them. There were two men and two women. The men were dark-haired. One woman was blonde and the other had extraordinarily beautiful, silky, brown hair. She was about five-nine in heels, had gray-green eyes and milky white skin. She wore a black satin dress with thin straps. I think they're called spaghetti straps."

"Did you know her?"

"Well," he joked, "a little better than I knew the others. She's the one I spoke with. Did I tell you I spoke with her?"

"Yes you did. Sir," the officer said, raising the yellow tape, "would you come with me please?"

"Where are we going, Officer?" Warren asked nervously as he ducked under the tape.

"Just over there," he said, escorting him to where two plainclothesmen were chatting.

"I'm Detective Riley," announced the stockier one, "and this is my partner, Detective Rourke. I understand you spoke to one of the people involved in the shooting."

"I did? I mean, I did! Uh, what do you mean, involved in the shooting? The young woman . . . was she shot? I mean, how was she involved?"

"This young woman," Detective Riley asked, appraising Warren's demeanor, "how well did you know her?"

"Well, I know she was quite stunning," Warren joshed uneasily.

"*Was* quite stunning?" the detective asked.

"Is . . . I meant *is* . . . *is* quite stunning," Warren trailed off as he watched Detective Riley jot something in his notepad. "She still *is*, I hope . . . isn't she? I mean, the woman in the black satin dress is not the one who was . . . ?"

"I'm sorry, sir, but we can't give out any information at this time."

"I understand, Officer, but someone said that there was a death and—"

"Sir, I suggest you go home!"

Warren did not go home as the detective suggested but retreated to a vantage point across the street behind a black utility vehicle. He waited nervously to see who would be loaded onto the gurney that was being wheeled into the restaurant. When the gurney finally emerged, it confirmed that someone had been killed, but a sheet covering the body made gender identification difficult.

"It looks like a man's body," Warren offered hopefully to the tattooed, T-shirted man standing next to him.

"It looks like a broad to me," the man responded as the gurney turned. "See the tits?"

"That may not be a bosom," Warren countered. "It could be a man with his arms folded."

"Yeah," the man conceded, "or a woman with her arms folded. I got five bucks says it's a broad!"

"You're on!" Warren shouted impulsively, hoping his confidence would influence the outcome.

"Now we'll never know," the betting man sighed, watching the gurney being slid into the ambulance.

"Yes we will!" shouted Warren on seeing his black-satined goddess emerge from the restaurant. "There she is!"

"There who is?" the bettor asked.

"The girl who wasn't on the stretcher!" Warren shouted.

"Look, mister, I didn't say nothing about no particular girl being on that stretcher. If you want to call off the bet—"

Warren left the man in midharangue and trotted across the street toward an officer who was shepherding "his girl" into a police car. On seeing the handsome couple being escorted to another car, Warren deduced that it was his girl's blind date who was dead. She is available, he concluded, and hopefully not a murderess.

The police car carrying "his girl" made a sharp U-turn and stopped a foot from where Warren stood. She turned her head and looked right into his face. With all that had gone on, he did not expect her to recognize him and was stunned to see her eyes light up and have her point excitedly at him. Through the windows, he could hear her muffled voice shouting, "That's him! That's him! That's the man I told you about!"

Before Warren knew what was happening, the front passenger door swung open and an officer, with a drawn gun, ordered him to put his hands on his head. While being handcuffed and frisked, Warren insisted on asking, "What the hell is this all about?," only to be told that anything he said might be used against him in a court of law and that he had a right to an attorney.

On learning, during his interrogation at the police station, that he was suspected of being an accessory to a murder, Warren decided to call upon his former law partner, Sam Guilder.

Both he and Sam Guilder agreed that there was no possible way he could be implicated in the murder of this Yuri Gregorivitch.

"Now where did you first meet Laura?" Sam asked.

"LAURA?" Warren asked, hearing her name for the first time. "Her name is Laura?"

"Laura Silte," Sam offered.

"Laura," Warren whispered, humming the first eight bars of the haunting song "Laura," the perfect name for the girl who had stolen his heart.

By telling the whole embarrassing truth, Warren had no trouble convincing his friend that he knew nothing about the death of the man known as Yuri "The Fury" Gregorivich. Laura Silte, like himself, was considered to have aided and abetted the crime.

After being released, Warren decided that he had to contact Laura Silte. The voice on the phone that said hello was even more seductive than he remembered and he asked if she would meet him for a drink.

"You want me to meet you for a drink?" she purred.

"I would consider it an honor if you would," he replied gallantly.

"Why, thank you, kind sir," she sang softly.

His cheeks flushed when he heard her add, "Under the circumstances, don't you think it would be wiser if we met in my apartment rather than at a bar?"

"Oh yes," he agreed, "much wiser."

Over a glass of *blanc de blanc,* Warren learned that Laura Silte had no idea that her blind date Yuri "The Fury"

Gregorivich was a drug dealer or that the people who had arranged for her to dine with him were engineering his execution.

"Oh my god!" was all Warren could offer, and he offered it many times as the story unfolded.

"I was told that as soon as we sat down," Laura continued, "I should drop my napkin and a waiter would pick it up. They said it was a little joke they were playing on Yuri because he was always dropping his napkin and had once tipped a waiter ten dollars for picking it up. So I was supposed to tip the waiter ten dollars after he picked up my napkin. They said it would make him laugh. I thought it was silly, but I'm a good sport so I dropped the napkin; but before the waiter could get to the table, there you were, Mr. . . . ."

"Warren Waits . . . uh, why don't you call me Warren?"

"Why, thank you, kind sir!" she sang.

Warren melted on hearing those five words come out of her sweet mouth.

"Well, when Yuri didn't laugh," she continued, "I thought it was because I hadn't given you the ten-dollar tip! A few minutes after you left, I saw a waiter looking at me, so I dropped the napkin again and the waiter picked it up. When I offered him the ten dollars, Yuri started to laugh. He was laughing so hard that when the waiter shot him in the head, the laugh, like, froze on his face. It was surreal."

"You must have been terrified," Warren said, grimacing.

"I was shaking like a leaf," she admitted. "There was blood splattered all over the elderly couple sitting at the table behind Yuri. It was gruesome!"

"I would imagine," Warren said, shuddering at the thought of a man's head being blown off. "You're a very brave young lady."

"Why, thank you, kind sir!"

Her using that phrase in this instance seemed a tad inappropriate, but it still made him quiver.

"Well, Laura," Warren said, raising his wineglass, "one good thing came out of all this. It gave me the chance to clink my glass against yours and say, 'To us.'"

"Why, thank you, kind sir!" she crooned, touching her glass to his. "Another good thing," she said, smiling and sipping the wine, "is that I found out about the new agency I just joined."

"Your agency?"

"Yes, Roberta Towers Fashion Models."

"I should have known," he said, snapping his fingers. "You're a model!"

"Well, I like to think I am. The last few assignments the agency sent me on were strange though. All my clients were Russians."

"Russian fashion designers?"

"I doubt it," Laura sneered. "They were really a pretty gross lot. Most of them had names I couldn't pronounce. I tell you, I was happy to say good night to those gentlemen. Now this Yuri, I thought he was cute. I was kind of

looking forward to spending the evening with him. But
. . . well, that's the way it goes sometimes. Life is full of
surprises."

"Yes it is," Warren sighed, shaking his head. "Laura,"
he continued hesitantly, "I hope I'm not out of line, but
from the first moment I saw you, I've wanted to ask you
something . . ."

"Oh? What is that?" she asked, cocking her head.

"Would you go to bed with me?" he asked simply.

"Oh yes, Warren," she gushed, "and happily."

"Oh that's wonderful, Laura! . . . Uh, one more question, and I hope I don't embarrass myself, but would I
have to pay you?"

"Nooo, nooooo," she laughed, squeezing his hand.
"This one is on me. In fact," she said, retrieving a bill
from her purse, "I'll give you the ten dollars I was supposed to give the waiter."

"Besides being the most beautiful woman I've ever
met," he said, taking the bill from her and putting it back
into her purse, "you are also the most generous."

"Why, thank you, kind sir!"

———————————

As Laura slept, snuggled in his arms, Warren looked over
at the chair where, hours before, he had carelessly
thrown the spaghetti-strap dress after helping her out of
it. He brushed her soft, white shoulder with his lips,
hoping she would awaken. He could not wait to ask her

the question that had been careening around in his brain ever since he had learned that she was a paid escort. He was sure that, given the choice, *any* woman, or nine hundred and ninety-nine thousand nine hundred and ninety-nine out of a *million*, would happily give up a career as a prostitute to become the wife of an appellate court judge.

On the drive home, Judge Warren Waits smiled sadly and muttered, "That girl is one in a million . . . *one* in a million . . ."

For the next three years Laura and the judge met for dinner at least twice a week and spent the night together in his apartment. One evening, after a delicious rack of lamb dinner that she had cooked, Laura raised her wineglass and announced that she was ready for marriage.

The following week, without being asked to sign a prenuptial agreement, Laura Silte married John Quincy McMellon, a very elderly and wealthy philanthropist. Often, in the past, Laura and Warren, in the heat of passion, would declare their love for each other. Warren had always doubted Laura's sincerity. Now, at last, his doubts were put to rest. After becoming Mrs. McMellon, not only did Laura continue to visit Warren regularly, but she steadfastly refused to accept any money for her time.

Geoff and Kurt

"I BEG your pardon, sir, but what is it that you're eating? My wife and I are about to order and that dish of yours looks awfully good."

"Oh, thank you. Is good. *Hassenpfeffer,* uh, rabbit. See on the menu, *lapin Provençale.* Very good flavors. You are American?"

"English."

"Ah, that is nice. We are from Germany. Emma and Kurt Kessler."

"How do you do? Alice and Geoff Hardwicke here."

"Mr. and Mrs. Hardwicke, how do you do? My wife, Emma, and I, we are going to England Tuesday. You know Harrow?"

"Well, how about that, darling? The Kesslers are going to Harrow."

"You are familiar with Harrow, Mr. Hardwicke?"

"Call me Geoff. Are we ever. Harrow is where Alice and I make our home."

"Unbelievable! There is where Emma and I go to visit."

"That *is* a jolly coincidence. Have you been there before?"

"Oh no, but my father spoke often of Harrow. During the World War he dropped bombs on it."

"You don't say!"

"Ah yes, twelve times."

"Alice, isn't that remarkable? Mr. Kessler's father bombed our hometown twelve times."

"Please to call me Kurt."

"Kurt, where are you folks from? Not Dresden, by any chance?"

"No, no. We are from Dortmund."

"That would be too big a coincidence. You see, in 1944 my dad dropped firebombs on Dresden."

"Your father firebombed Dresden? No, I don't believe it!"

"It's true. His squadron sent the whole city up in flames."

"I know, I know, that is the reason why my family moved to Dortmund."

"Alice, isn't this an astonishing coincidence?!"

"Mind-boggling!"

"Mr. Hardwicke—I'm sorry, Geoff—may I buy you a bottle of wine?"

"I was about to ask you that, Kurt."

"*Ach,* but I ask first."

"Ah yes, but we won the war!"

"And you win again. All right, Geoff, you buy the wine!"

Heshie and Joey

HESHIE AND JOEY came out of their respective apartment buildings at precisely the same moment. It was almost as if a bell had rung summoning them out of their stuffy old tenements and into the fresh morning air. Heshie's side of Belmont Avenue was bathed in bright sunlight, while Joey's side would remain shaded until late afternoon. Neither boy appeared to acknowledge the other's existence. They sneaked looks but turned away before being caught. Each was trying to determine if the other could be a potential best friend. Neither had one—Joey, because he had just moved into the neighborhood, and Heshie, because "he smelled funny." On the boat from Hungary, when he was four years old, he had developed a mysterious skin condition that required smearing his face with a thick, foul-smelling, yellowish salve. Dominic DeStefano had once announced to his kid brother, Carmelo, that his new Jewish friend smelled like "a camphor ball dipped in shit" and "to get him the hell out of the house."

Carmelo, who suffered from an allergy that kept his

nose stuffed up for most of the year, had no idea what his tyrant brother was talking about. All he knew was that Heshie was a nice, quiet kid with a funny accent and could build incredible things with his erector set. When Carmelo refused to give up his friend, Dominic took it upon himself to tell Heshie that he was "stinking up the joint" and to "take a hike and never come back!" Heshie ran home crying and vowed that he would never play with Carmelo again even if he got down on his knees and begged him "a million million times."

It was three lonely weeks before Heshie saw a potential playmate, sitting on the stoop, across the street, looking as if he needed a friend as much as Heshie did.

Heshie decided that since he had lived in the neighborhood longer, it was up to him to make the first move.

"I have a football," Heshie shouted, holding up his bright red rubber football. "Would you like to play catch with me?"

Being myopic, Joey had trouble catching a ball but was aching to make a friend, even one who spoke with a Hungarian accent.

"Okay," Joey shouted back, "shall I come across the street to you or you wanna come over here?"

Heshie, having just been freshly coated with the smelly salve, wanted to keep as much distance as possible between him and his new playmate.

"We'll throw the ball across the street," Heshie shouted. "Can you throw that far?"

Joey, never having thrown a football, shrugged and said that he didn't know.

"Don't worry, it's easy," Heshie assured Joey, gripping the ball. "You ready?"

Joey was not at all ready, but shouted that he was. Heshie reared back and, with all his might, threw the ball far over Joey's head. It hit the redbrick wall of Joey's apartment house and bounced crazily halfway back across the street.

"I'm a really strong thrower and I threw it too hard," Heshie explained, darting into the street to retrieve the ball. "This time, I won't throw it so hard. Ready?"

"Ready," Joey lied, hoping that Heshie would throw the ball through a window so they would be done playing catch.

Heshie cocked his arm and threw a perfect pass. Joey stood transfixed and watched the red rubber football flying toward him at what seemed like the speed of light. Before he could decide whether to duck and let it hit the wall again, the tip of the ball spiraled into the right lens of his new glasses. The football and the eyeglasses went flying into the air. Joey fell to his knees and covered his eyes.

"Why didn't you catch it?" Heshie asked pleadingly. "It was a great pass, right to you!"

"My eyes, my eyes," Joey howled, a drop of blood visible on his finger. "I can't see! I can't see!"

Realizing that the game was over, Heshie ran into the

street, gathered up his football, and barely avoided getting hit by a car. Racing up the four flights to his apartment, he could hear Joey's voice hysterically pleading for his mother to rescue him. As Heshie pounded at the door for someone to let him in, he heard the faint echo of Joey's voice screaming, "Maamaaaa . . . I'm bliiind!!"

Heshie alternated ringing the bell and pounding on the door until his mother finally opened it. Sobbing, he threw his arms around her ample thighs and buried his head in her stomach in a futile attempt to return to the safety of her womb.

Hannah Hirsh had three other children, but Heshie was her jewel.

"What is it, my darling?" she asked, her voice calm and reassuring. "Tell Mama what happened."

With his face burrowing into his mother's apron, Heshie could manage only a few gurgles and sobs.

"What is it, darling?" Hannah asked again, stroking his head and speaking Hungarian. "Nothing could be so bad."

"It is!" Heshie sobbed, choking on his spittle. "The . . . the new boy . . . from . . . across . . . the street . . . he . . . he—"

"He said you smelled bad," Hannah offered, trying to finish his sentence for him, "and he didn't want to play with you . . . ?"

"Nooo," he exploded, raising his head and leaving a yellow salve stain on her flowered apron, "I hit . . . him . . .

in his glasses with my football . . . and I . . . I made him blind!"

"Now, now," Hannah responded, "with a rubber football, you can't make someone blind."

"Yes, you can!" Heshie shouted at the top of his lungs. "I threw it with all my might. Papa yelled at me for throwing the ball so hard at David. He said I could take his eye out."

"Heshie, darling, David is only three and Papa didn't really mean that you could take his eye out. That's just an expression."

No matter how hard Hannah tried, Heshie refused to be consoled. He was certain that he would be arrested and sent to jail. His uncle Louis had often told him stories about bad boys who had been sent to jail for much lesser offenses.

Clutching his little red football, Heshie ran sobbing into the bedroom and immediately stifled a sob when he saw his baby brother napping peacefully. Taking someone's eye out and waking up a sleeping kid brother were too many punishable acts for one day. He tiptoed into the closet, quietly shut the door, and settled himself on a bundle of old clothes that his mother was saving to send to the poor people in Europe. He hoped that when the police came to look for him, they wouldn't think of looking here.

Hannah let Heshie be. She knew her son. If she did not seem to be worried about what he had done, sooner or later he would feel that he was not in as much trouble as he thought. When suppertime arrived and his mother sang out sweetly, "Heshie, darling, wash up and come in for supper, we're all waiting," Heshie felt safe enough to venture out of the closet.

He was surprised that during the meal no one mentioned anything about Joey or the football. He expected his older brother, Simon, or his sister, Marsha, to make some nasty remark. That his father was silent worried him, for it meant that a long lecture and some kind of disciplinary action was being planned for him after dinner. Morris Hirsh never did anything during dinner. If someone would accidentally broach a disturbing subject, Morris would raise his dinner knife and remind that person, *"Az meir est meir est!"* And, for emphasis, he'd repeat it in English: "When one eats, one eats!"

Three-year-old David, who didn't understand the rules, asked, "Heshie, ball? Me play ball?"

Heshie glanced quickly at his father, sure that David's allusion to the "weapon" would open the floodgates.

"David, no play ball at supper," Hannah sang out in her sweetest soprano. "Eat your nice carrots."

Only after his father had finished his serving of raspberry Jell-O did he address Heshie's problem.

"Heshie," Morris said, wiping his mouth, "Mama tells me that you played a very rough game of football today. Is that so?"

Heshie nodded and worried about what his father was

gearing up to say. Morris Hirsh was never brief and to the point. He had dreams of going to law school and becoming either Emile Zola or Clarence Darrow, but he was thwarted by a worldwide depression, a marriage, four children, and the inability to read or write English.

"Heshie," his father said, in Hungarian, "the little boy you played catch with, have you spoken to him since you hit him in the eye?"

Heshie shook his head.

"Don't you think you should speak to him?"

Again, Heshie shook his head.

"Wouldn't you like to apologize and find out how he is?"

Heshie shook his head violently three times.

"Heshie," Morris said, rising from the table, "I think that you should speak to him. Come," he ordered, taking Heshie's hand, "we'll ask the janitor across the street what apartment the new people moved into and we'll talk to them."

As Heshie was led off, he looked to his mother for sympathy, which she gave him with a smile.

Mr. Mitchell, the janitor who spoke with a heavy Jamaican accent, was able, after three attempts, to make Morris understand that the new tenants were the Goodelmans and were living in apartment twenty-seven on the second floor. Heshie's heart started to race when he realized that he would soon be confronted by a one-eyed boy he had made that way. Morris rang the doorbell twice and was about to ring it again when he heard slow, shuffling footsteps approaching the door. Heshie held his father's large calloused hand tightly, and imagined the crippled monster in the ghost story his brother Simon insisted on telling at bedtime whenever there was a thunderstorm.

"Closer, closer," Simon would intone, "the monster came closer and closer."

As the Goodelman door slowly opened, Heshie let out an audible yelp. He imagined the ghost grabbing him by the head and shouting, "An eye for an eye!," a phrase he had heard his uncle Louis use many times in heated political discussions with his father.

Heshie was only slightly relieved to see a white-haired ancient Jewish grandma peer at them through the crack.

"Yes, what is it?" she piped in a high-pitched voice. "Nobody's home, come back later. I'm here all alone. Are you a friend of Jake's? He's not here. Sarah is also not here, they both took Joey to the hospital . . . he was bleeding . . . I'm worried . . . it was five, six hours ago . . . they should be back already . . . you heard what happened? Are you from the police department? I told them to call the police and find out what happened and who the boy is . . .

"Is that the boy, Officer?" the old woman shouted, seeing Heshie trying to duck behind his father. "You caught him! Good, good! You should be put in jail," she cackled, pointing a bony witchlike finger at the cowering

Heshie. "A boy does such a terrible thing! What did Joey ever do to you? Officer, why did you bring him here? The rotten hooligan! What kind of family do you come from . . . throwing a baseball into a boy's eye?"

Heshie wanted to correct her, but feared that telling her it was not a baseball but a *foot*ball would only incriminate him. He was glad his father spoke up. Morris had been trying to stop the old woman's rambling monologue, but she hadn't been aware that he was talking. Her cataracts allowed her to see only fuzzy images and she could hear nothing softer than a gunshot.

Morris patiently and loudly explained that Heshie was his son and that they were there to pay their respects and to offer any help they could. Heshie was surprised and happy to see how unruffled his father was when the old lady slammed the door in his face.

"She's very old," his father explained, "and sometimes old people get things a little mixed up. We'll come back later."

That night Heshie went to bed with both his mother's and his father's guarantee that everything was going to be all right. No policeman would come to take him to jail and Joey Goodelman was not going to be blind. Armed with these positive images, Heshie fell asleep during the second chorus of Brahms's lullaby. Hannah sang all her children to sleep until they considered the ritual too babyish. Heshie, at six and a half, was not nearly ready to cancel the nightly lullaby.

Despite his mother's gentleness and assurances, Heshie went through a full schedule of nightmares that night. Among them he dreamed that a witch, resembling Grandma Goodelman, was chasing him up a long, long flight of stairs, waving a big football covered with a red-and-yellow salve. He dreamed too that his uncle Louis was trying to poke his eyes out with a toothpick. Just as his uncle was about the gouge him, Heshie awoke screaming, which woke up his baby brother, which in turn brought Hannah into their room. She hushed and patted the crying baby as she held Heshie in her arms and told him that tonight she would allow him to sleep in the big bed with Mama and Papa. A peaceful Heshie lay between his parents, safe from policemen, witches, and his uncle Louis.

At six-thirty that morning, Heshie's reverie was broken by the sound of the door buzzer.

"Who's ringing so early?" Hannah asked.

"I'll open the door and see," Morris answered.

"I'll go with you," she volunteered.

Heshie, awakened by the buzzer and sensing danger, pulled the covers over his head, burrowed his way down to the foot of the bed, and balled himself up into the smallest person he could be. He prayed his parents would not give him away to the police.

It was not the police, but Joey's father, Jacob Goodelman.

"I'm sorry if I woke you but I'm on my way to

work," he explained, "and I wanted to speak with you before tonight."

Hearing that it was not the police, Heshie slid out of bed and peeked around the bedroom door. Mr. Goodelman did not seem angry when he described how he and his wife had taken Joey to the emergency ward to have two stitches put in above his right eyebrow. Heshie's initial feelings of guilt and fear turned quickly to pride when he heard Mr. Goodelman praising him.

"That young man of yours must have a very strong arm. It was a pretty deep cut."

Morris agreed that his son had a strong arm and offered to pay for the glasses Heshie had broken.

"Pay me?" Mr. Goodelman laughed. "I should pay you."

"Why should you pay me, Mr. Goodelman? That doesn't make sense."

Mr. Goodelman explained that Joey had an astigmatism in both eyes and when Heshie hit Joey in his right eye, it realigned something and cured the astigmatism.

"I asked the doctor," Mr. Goodelman chuckled. "Maybe I should have your boy hit Joey in the other eye too."

The whole Hirsh family roared at this, Heshie roaring the loudest even though the joke escaped him.

New glasses were ordered and Mr. Goodelman was happy to pay for them. Heshie's perfect pass had improved Joey's eyesight by 40 percent.

"So, Heshie," Mr. Goodelman suggested, "you think maybe when you and Joey play catch again, he'll be able to catch your spiral bullet?"

"Maybe," Heshie agreed, "if I don't throw my speedy spiral right away."

Joey and Heshie did play catch again, and they did become best friends. Surprisingly, Joey was not revolted by the odor of Heshie's salve. He said it smelled like the winter coats that hung in the hall closet.

Joey and Heshie played together every day for five years. When the Goodelmans moved to Forest Hills they played together once a month on the Sundays Joey and the Goodelmans came to visit Grandma, who had refused to leave the Bronx and "become a burden." After Grandma died, the boys would play together every summer for two weeks when the Goodelmans invited Heshie to be their guest at their beach house in Far Rockaway. When the Goodelmans moved to Phoenix so Joey's mother could spend her remaining years in a dry climate, they wrote to each other fairly often, then less often, then not at all . . .

———————————

In a small restaurant in Strassburg, France, Harold Hirsh and Joe Goodleman sat with their wives, at adjoining tables. Thirty-nine years had passed since they'd last met. They had traded glances but neither recognized the bald, paunchy person he saw as being anyone he knew.

They might never have connected if Harold's wife, Lucille, had not decried her husband's choice of dessert.

"Tarte Tatin?" she asked angrily. "Are you crazy?"

"It's apples, honey," he argued.

"Apples?" she mocked. "*One* apple, one pound of butter, and one pound of sugar. Heshie, are you trying to make me a widow?"

Joey spun around and looked at the man called Heshie and asked, "Heshie Hirsh?"

It took no longer than a nanosecond for Heshie to recognize the gray-haired man as his old best friend Joey Goodelman. The two men embraced warmly, introduced their wives, passed around photos of their grandchildren, and traded stories about their recent hospitalizations. To celebrate their reunion and their recovery from successful bypass surgery they ordered, "One Tarte Tatin and four forks." Heshie insisted that the dessert be put on his bill, arguing, "I owe it to you. Your pop wouldn't let us pay for the glasses I broke."

Two solid hours of good feelings, good conversation, and happy reminiscences ended with an agreement to "do this again, real soon." Before leaving the table, Harold Hirsh and Joe Goodelman exchanged telephone numbers and promised to keep in touch and, because their wives thought it a good idea, they actually did.

Caz

"Ah, Caz, my good and dear friend, you look fit, I trust that you are well."

"But for a dull ache in my groin, Vittorio, I can truthfully say that I am in the best shape of my life."

"And how do you find your new lady friend?"

"Smashing and available at all hours."

"As I would expect. What is her name?"

"I am not sure. I meant to ask her last night but I was distracted."

"Well, as Shakespeare says, 'What's in a name?' By the way, Gina and I are picnicking tomorrow. Care to join us?"

"I would adore that, Vittorio, but I have this bothersome groin thing."

"How long have you had it?"

"I believe it started immediately after Valentine's Day."

"Caz, Valentine's day was six months ago. Have you seen a physician?"

"Why would I?"

"My god, Caz, if I had a pain that long, I would want to know what was causing it."

"I do know that I carried this rather heavy young lady up a long flight of marble stairs . . . perhaps . . . no, no. I already had the pain before I lifted her off the floor . . ."

"Why don't you see a doctor?"

"Because I know this pain will go away . . . as they all do. The body has a way of healing itself . . ."

"Caz, in case your body does not know that way, my cousin Dr. Roncalo is an excellent diagnostician. You should get at least one professional opinion."

———————————

"Dr. Roncalo, I cannot believe what you are suggesting. Except for that one little groin pain, I feel wonderful."

"But you say the pain is constant and is getting worse daily."

"But it is not unbearable."

"It will become so unless you accept what must be done."

"Doctor, what you are prescribing is so drastic. Is there not a pill? Or perhaps you could operate? I hear there are new surgical procedures—"

"There are no new procedures for your condition, and what I am recommending is not that extreme."

"NOT that EXTREME, you say? Giving up sex is NOT that EXTREME?"

"Signor Casanova, please do not shout. I did not ask you to give up sex, I merely recommended that you cut back—"

"TO THREE TIMES A NIGHT AND NO MORN-ING OR AFTERNOON DALLIANCES ON SUN-DAY?! Doctor, that to me is giving it up! I cannot live that way. I would rather suffer the pain."

"It is your life, Signor."

"Thank you, Doctor, I am glad you agree."

Casanova died on February 14, 1798. Last week, on the two-hundredth anniversary of his death, an autopsy was performed and the coroner found that the pain in his groin was still measurable.

As Easy as ABC

THE RADIO ALARM clicked on and blared out the last six bars of the *Eroica* Symphony. Leo Fromm was jolted awake and sat bolt upright in his bed. Without checking the time, he started to put on the same underwear, socks, jeans, and flannel work shirt he had worn the day before. He could not afford to lose a minute of valuable time searching his room for fresher clothes, if indeed there were any. Leo had had a particularly bad Sunday, and he knew that he would have to work that much harder today. Things were getting out of hand and he vowed that this Monday he would turn them around. This was the fourth weekend in a row he had committed to his work. He brushed his teeth with a dry brush, then sucked a mouthful of water from the faucet, trying unsuccessfully to rinse away his morning mouth odor. He shoved a couple of pencil stubs into his pocket, grabbed a worn composition workbook from under his unmade bed, and made his way out of the cluttered apartment.

Leo walked briskly down the four flights of stairs, trying to decide where he might be most successful in accomplishing the day's work. He had worked Times Square all day Friday, Saturday, and Sunday without improving his lot one bit. In fact, he had lost ground. He had worked himself into a position where only a miracle could extricate him from total disaster. Last night, as he'd sat on his bed eating his last chocolate chip cookie, he had vowed he would try just one more time.

The new shopping mall might be the answer; it had to be. For a moment, he thought of pretending to be blind and asking a stranger to lead him to the mall. This way he would not see posters and signs that might get him deeper in trouble, but he decided that it would be unfair, it was not the way he played the game. It would be cheating, and he would not be able to face himself if he had cheated.

He opened his book, the same classic school workbook with the black-and-white mottled design on the stiff cardboard cover that he had used in grammar school. The workbook he was poring over now was the hundredth one he had bought since leaving school. He had never dreamed, when he started this project in the fourth grade, that it would become his whole life. He never envisioned the burdensome responsibility he was taking on. He remembered well the first words he had written in his workbook. He was seated in the auditorium during a school assembly and happened to glance up at the "Exit" sign. He jotted down the letters, *E X I T*, on the back page of his workbook and decided that these letters would have to remain there until he could find an *E*, an *X*, an *I*, and a *T* to cancel out the original letters he had written down. He was thrilled to have invented a game, a diversion he could use to beat the tremendous boredom he tried vainly to fight off in all of his classes. At first he thought it too simple a game because within seconds of writing the letters *E X I T* in his book, he noticed another exit sign to the left of the stage. He quickly crossed out each letter and was even. Staying even was the sole object of the game. He decided it could be great fun and, for a while, it was. He found that the greater the challenge, the greater the exhilaration when he met the challenge and won. His first major triumph came in the first week when he owed himself the letters he had collected from a "No Smoking" sign. Within a short time he had found a restaurant called King's Moon. It was perfect. The *K i n g* of the sign would cancel out the second syllable of Smo*king*. The *S* of *Smoking* would cancel out the *S* in King'*s*. The *mo* of S*mo*king and the letters in *No* would be canceled by the letters in the word *Moon*. All he owed himself was an apostrophe, which he felt confident he would find.

Had he known what the future of the game held for him, he might have quit, but he couldn't think of quitting now.

He made his way to the mall, burying his attention in

his notebook, thereby avoiding any signs or posters that would add new letters to his burgeoning list. He already owed himself dozens upon dozens of letters and punctuation marks, among them too many of the very difficult ones to find, the Q's, the Z's, and the X's. The canceling of Z's, he knew, must be his first priority.

He rode the elevator to the fourth floor, where he read that a new Sleep Shop had opened. He prayed there would be that mattress ad he had once seen that promised a potential buyer, "Hour upon Hour of Happy ZZZZZ's!" He needed those ZZZZZ's. A month earlier he had been badly burnt when, passing a parking lot, he had seen a fleet of "ZZBEST" carpet-cleaning trucks lined up and ready to roll. He was tempted to cheat and have one truck's logo cancel the next one's, but from his angle he saw the whole fleet in a single glance. He had to list all the letters, which included the nettlesome Z's.

He approached the Sleep Shop, drew a deep breath, and looked up. He could not believe his luck. In the window were two mannequins asleep in a king-size bed. Over each of their heads a cartoon balloon was suspended, with more Z's than he could count. The Z's were in diminishing sizes and the last few were so small that they were barely decipherable. He assumed that even the most minuscule, which was little more than a dot, was a Z and he would use it. He had taken credit for twenty-eight of them and all but wiped out his Z debt. He felt his heart racing as he crossed off the last of the Z's. He looked up quickly and, with ferretlike glances, he searched the window for more good fortune.

"Omigod," he shrieked as his eyes lit upon the display in the adjoining window: "Queen-size beds and Quilts for the Queenliest Queens in the Queendom." Five *Q*'s! He immediately struck out five of the *Q*'s on his list, then five *U*'s, and all the *E*'s, *S*'s, *N*'s, and *T*'s, and one last *Z*. He filled his lungs with air and found himself smiling for the first time in months. The day had started as he had prayed it would. He needed this kind of bonanza.

For the rest of the day, Leo Fromm went from store to store checking signs, posters, and advertisements and managed to cancel out two-thirds of the letters he owed himself. At the Quadraplex Theaters, the marquees took care of another raft of letters.

It was close to nine o'clock when he made his way out of the mall. He had picked up a few new letters, but by and large he had done better than he had in years. If he could keep from picking up any more before he got home, he knew that with one more day like today, he would be even. He kept his eyes on his worn Adidas as he raced down the street to the bus stop, trying to avoid seeing candy wrappers and parts of newspapers. His goal, which had eluded him all these years, was to get even, 100 percent even. To have in his book not one letter or one apostrophe or one period to cross out. Then and only then would he close his book, put it in the closet with the dozens of others, and start living his life, a normal life. He would call his father in Boston and proudly inform him that he would not be needing his monthly allowance anymore. He would call his mother in Orlando and tell her he was now ready to work in her gift shop.

He began to fear that he might accidentally pick up some new letters if he kept his eyes open so he squinted just enough to blur out the world about him. He half-crossed his eyes as he boarded the bus and made his way to the back, where he found a seat. Now he could shut his eyes tight and block out everything. Leo Fromm was a very tired man and looked ten or fifteen years older than the thirty-five he was.

As the bus snaked its way down the crowded avenue, Leo found himself getting pleasantly drowsy. Before nodding off, he thought of the chocolate chip cookies he had received from his mother. He still had half a tinful and decided to give himself a party tonight and eat the rest.

"I deserve a party!" he announced loudly.

A few of his fellow passengers looked at him quizzically, but he was oblivious to them, as he had fallen into a deep sleep. He dreamed that in front of his apartment window a construction crane hoisted a huge billboard that had all the letters and punctuation marks that he owed himself. Then he heard a voice, a deep, hoarse, kindly voice not unlike his church's pastor's.

"My son, thou art troubled. I see it in thy face."

Leo's pastor had never addressed him as "My son," nor did he say, "thou" and "thy."

"A heavy burden rests on thy shoulders," the voice continued, "and thou wouldst have that weight lifted. I shall do this for thee for I am thy savior. Lift up thy head, open wide thine eyes, and see the gift I bring thee."

Leo Fromm "opened wide his eyes" and beheld his bearded savior dressed in a soiled and tattered burlap robe. A crown of thorns fashioned of papier-mâché adorned his head. With dirt-encrusted hands, the savior thrust forward a large, grimy, cardboard placard.

"Read and be saved!" he bellowed.

Leo began to shake and sob as he read the hand-lettered message that filled every square inch of the placard.

> "Beelzebub, be gone! Be gone, Beelzebub!
> Thou shall not have my soul, zealot!
> Beelzebub, I exorcise thee, zealot!
> Out, Beelzebub! Zealot! Thou art exorcised!
> Out, Beelzebub! Zealot! Thou art exorcised!
> Out, Beelzebub! Zealot! Thou art exorcised!"

Leo was now committed to adding more *X*'s and *Z*'s than he had just stricken from his ledger. He knew he was doomed. He thought of shutting his eyes and forgetting what he'd seen, but his rules didn't allow that. Once he had committed to reading something, he had to enter all the letters. His vision blurred and his lungs starting to gasp for air, Leo hastily scribbled all the accursed *Z*'s and *X*'s into his book.

"Yes, my son," the bearded savior spoke, smiling beatifically at his newest convert, "record these words in your tablet, pass them on to other sinners and thou shalt enter the Kingdom of Heaven. Thou art saved!"

"Thou shalt enter the Kingdom of Heaven" were the last words Leo heard before keeling over and smashing his head on the floor of the bus.

———————————

Leo entered not the Kingdom of Heaven but the Wiseman-Jones Psychiatric Clinic in Pound Ridge, New York.

Every afternoon Leo sat placidly under a shady elm tree and stared at his empty hands. Every so often he would look over to where his mother and father were conversing with Dr. Isaac Jones. He could not hear what they were saying, nor did he care. He had more important things on his mind.

Dr. Jones was explaining to Leo's parents that in the four months of therapy Leo had had with his co-director, Dr. Wiseman, the doctor had achieved a remarkable understanding of their son's letter-matching obsession and had managed to dissuade him from asking for pads and pencils.

"I am quite certain," the doctor explained, "that Leo's silence is only temporary, and we are looking for a complete recovery. What you must decide in these next weeks is whether he goes to Boston with you, Mr. Fromm, or to Florida with you, Mrs. Wolczek. I think his seeing the two of you together has been most beneficial. He really seems to enjoy it. I noticed today how often he smiled when he looked at the two of you. It was most therapeutic."

Leo's mother and father visiting him conjointly was indeed therapeutic. It pleased Leo to note that his dad's two blue eyes canceled out his mom's two blue eyes and his dad's black oxford shoes canceled out his mom's black pumps and the tin of chocolate chip cookies that his mom had brought canceled out the bag of Famous Amos chocolate chip cookies that his dad had brought.

Leo felt blessed to have such perfectly matched parents.

The Heidi and Albert Correspondence

August 17, 1904

My dearest, darling Albert,

Oh, how I miss you! I wish you could have stayed the night. I am grateful, however, that you dozed for thirty blissful minutes. It gave me the opportunity to do something I was aching to do. I would have asked your permission, but I was afraid you would have refused me and thought me a silly ninny. Well, my big cuddly bear, if tomorrow one of your colleagues should say, "Professor, there's a clump of hair missing from the back of your head," you can say, "I know. An impetuous young woman who adores me snipped off the curl. She wanted it as a remembrance of the one glorious night we spent in each other's arms." Please don't be angry with me. Someday when you are a famous violinist, and I am certain you will be, I'll have this lock of hair to show to our child if, by a miracle, I become pregnant from our one night of ecstasy.

I know how much you love your wife so I do not expect that we will ever see each other again. I will cherish forever the three hours and ten minutes that you spent in my bed.

Eternally yours,

Heidi Baumheller

P.S. Enclosed is a scrap of paper I found beneath the chair where you hung your trousers. The dog must have chewed it. It looks like a $B = mc^2$, or it could be an $E = mc^2$ . . . is it important?

Aunt Delia and Her Twins

ORRIN TUTTLE felt confident that today was going to be a productive one. It was quickly confirmed when he saw a Federal Express van pull away from the curb and leave a parking space directly in front of the building where his new job interview was to take place. With a minimum amount of jockeying, he eased his BMW into the space.

Now, he thought, if I can just slip into this new job as smoothly.

He sprang from the car, strode to the parking meter, and extracted four coins from his pocket. Three nickels and a penny!

"Damnit!" he mumbled, loudly enough to startle an elderly gentlewoman.

"Damn what?" she asked, turning to him.

"I'm sorry," he explained, "I don't have quarters for the parking meter, and I have an important appointment in a few minutes. You wouldn't have change for a twenty-dollar bill, would you?"

"I think I do, young man," she said, opening her purse

while scanning Orrin's face. "If I'm not being too forward, may I ask your name?"

"Orrin Tuttle. Why do you ask?"

"It's uncanny, but you're the spitting image of my nephew Larry."

"That's interesting; uh, do you have the change?"

"I'm sure I do," she said, opening her wallet. "Oh, I'm so sorry, but it seems all I have are twenties and fifties; but there's a newsstand at the corner. I'm sure Jimmy will oblige you, he's very nice. I'll go with you. I know you're in a hurry but I won't hold you up. I'm a very brisk walker even though I'll be seventy-nine next Thursday. By the way, my name is Delia."

"How do you do, Delia?" he mumbled as he tried to pull away.

"As you can see, I do very well," she shouted, quickening her pace. "Actually, it's Cordelia, Cordelia West. My father was Jonathan West of West Industries."

"Oh yes. Well, it was nice to . . . ," he mumbled incoherently, hoping to end their relationship.

"We Wests are a hardy lot," she persisted. "Daddy lived to be ninety-nine but Uncles Franklin and Theodore, who made their home in California, passed on at eighty-five and eighty-eight. The West Coast Wests didn't fare as well as the East Coast Wests." She laughed at the little family joke that she made as often as she could.

The two arrived at the newsstand in a dead heat. While

Orrin was trying to catch his breath, Delia negotiated with the newsstand dealer.

"Jimmy, this gentleman needs change for a twenty-dollar bill. I'll vouch for the fact that it's a twenty!"

"Because Jimmy is blind," Delia explained, walking back to the car, "he is reluctant to make change for strangers."

Orrin put the quarters in the meter, thanked Delia sincerely for helping him, and apologized for seeming curt.

"Young man, I appreciate your sensitivity. Most young people today have little patience for older folk."

"Well," Orrin offered, "back in Gadsden, Alabama, we learned to respect our elders or else."

Orrin started for the building and got as far as the revolving door when he heard her call his name.

"Orrin, what kind of a job are you looking for?"

He knew he had to answer or risk being followed into the building.

"I'm being interviewed for an account executive position in an advertising firm."

"I don't believe it," she said, slapping her gloved hands together.

"I beg your pardon?"

"Is Tuttle your real name or were you by any chance adopted?"

If Delia had asked any other question but that, he might have wished her a "Good day" and bolted for the elevator.

"Mrs. West," he said, smiling, "that is a very unusual question to ask a stranger."

"Oh, I am aware of that. Were you adopted?"

"I must know why you ask me that."

"Well, Orrin, my nephew Larry West, who I said could be your twin, is not my natural nephew. My youngest brother, Sebastian, and his wife, Ardele, were not able to have children . . . medical problems that they never shared with me. In any event, they adopted this darling little baby, Larry, who so reminds me of you. Your hair color, the blue-green eyes, the height, the way you carry yourself, even your way of speaking. I hope you don't think I'm an addled old woman, but I assure you I have never walked up to another person and said I thought you were my nephew's twin, but good god, I think you are. Are you adopted?"

Orrin checked his watch and realized that in five minutes he would be late for his interview. He took Delia by the arm and led her into the building. He found a quiet corner in the marbled lobby and explained to her that it was a big joke in his family.

"I was constantly chided about being adopted. As you can see, I am six feet, three inches tall and blond, and both my parents are five feet three and dark."

"Did you never ask them if you were adopted?"

"Oh, sure, when I was fifteen years old and towered above them. They laughed and swore that I was their natural child and I should never, ever doubt it."

"Well, if you met my nephew Larry, you might."

"Your nephew knows he's adopted?"

"Oh, yes, but he doesn't know who his natural parents are. He's very eager to find them, and I must say that Sebastian and Ardele are very supportive of his desire to do so. They have given him all the information they have, and so far it has led nowhere. Did I mention that Larry is in advertising?"

"No, you didn't."

"He's the director of the commercial art department at Bigelow and Smutz."

"Oh my god, I used to work for Bigelow and Smutz, my first job."

"I know."

"How could you?"

"When Larry started there last fall, an old maintenance man told Larry how there was this tall, young, blond man who used to work there who looked a lot like him. It had to be you."

"Mrs. West," Orrin asked, inhaling deeply, "could you arrange for us to meet?"

Orrin's head was spinning. He handed Delia a business card and told her to call him later that day. Cordelia West found herself smiling as she watched the dazed young man walk slowly toward the elevators.

During the interview with Samuel Simmons of Simmons, Paltrow, and Scott, Orrin kept imagining himself as a twin. He was plainly distracted but somehow managed to keep enough of his personality intact to impress Mr. Simmons. The job was his if he wanted it.

"Orrin, this is your aunt Delia," Orrin heard on his answering machine when he arrived home. "I know I'm being premature calling myself your aunt, but Larry is coming to dinner tonight and I'm hoping you'll join us."

Orrin jotted down the address and time and then considered his options. He realized he had none. He had to see this Larry and find out if his folks had lied to him.

Orrin found it difficult deciding what to wear for this occasion.

"Hey, Tuttle," he addressed himself in the mirror, "you're not going to a wedding, you're going to meet someone who may look like you . . ."

He opted for the outfit he had worn all day. If it was good enough to land a high-paying job, it was good enough for this weird dinner date.

Knowing the parking problems he would be dealing with at Fifth Avenue and Seventy-eighth Street, Orrin chose to leave himself a cushion of time. Since today seemed to be his day, he was not surprised to find a spot just two car lengths from the canopied entrance to Delia's apartment building.

As Orrin approached the entrance, the red-uniformed doorman tipped his cap.

"Evening, Mr. Tuttle," he said, opening the ornate brass door. "You do look like Mrs. West's nephew

Larry," he explained, reading the puzzled look on Orrin's face. "She said to go right up."

Orrin smiled and allowed himself to be ushered through the lobby and into the elevator.

"Orrin!" Delia sang out as her butler opened the door. "I'm so glad you came early. Larry did too. He can't wait to meet you. I reached him at his girlfriend's home in East Hampton and he helicoptered in this morning."

Delia took Orrin by the hand and led him down a long hall. She informed him that his "twin" was in the library eagerly awaiting their rendezvous. Larry was in the process of pouring a vintage pinot noir into a wine-glass when they arrived.

"Larry, darling," Delia gushed, "I want you to meet Orrin Tuttle, and, Orrin, this is my favorite nephew, Larry West."

They mumbled inaudible hellos and exchanged firm handshakes. All three members of the summit meeting stood silently for a long moment, Orrin and Larry studying each other and Delia studying them both.

"It's absolutely uncanny, how much you look alike. Don't you both feel as if you're looking into a mirror?"

They turned slowly to look at Delia.

"Oh, gracious," she shouted, "I've read how twins, even if they were separated at birth, will do things like that."

"Like what?" Larry asked.

"Like you and Orrin just did, turning to look at me at exactly the same time."

"Aunt Delia, you asked us a question and we naturally turned to you."

"Yes, but at precisely the same moment and with precisely the same expression on your faces."

Larry and Orrin turned to each other and smiled.

"There!" Delia pointed out, "you did it again, same head turn, same smile, and now you're both shaking your heads the same way. Twins do that. I know I'm right about you two!"

"Aunt Delia," Larry demurred, "as much as you seem to want us to be twins, I don't think Orrin and I are."

"I have to agree with Larry." Orrin said, "Oh, there is a sort of resemblance, but not as you described."

Delia collapsed into an easy chair and shook her head sadly.

"I was so sure you two looked like twins. I must be getting anile."

"Aunt Delia, if I can be honest, your problem is not anility, it's vanity. If you would just put on your glasses, you would see what *is* and not what you wish things to be."

"Oh, I guess you're right, as always, Larry," Celia sighed, picking up a crystal dinner bell and shaking it vigorously. "Why don't we make the best of my silly little farrago and enjoy the rest of this evening? I've had cook prepare us a lovely dinner. Your favorite, Larry, POULET VINAIGRE."

"Vinegar chicken!" Orrin said, his voice rising half an octave. "I love vinegar chicken!"

"Are you saying that to be a good guest?" Larry asked, smiling.

"No, no. My college roommate's mother was French, she made it every time I asked her to."

"Well, there you are," snapped Delia. "I knew there was something about you two!"

"Orrin, perhaps we are related. Maybe first cousins."

"I'd say more likely second cousins," Orrin countered, staring at Larry's face.

"Yes," Larry answered, putting his hand on Orrin's chin and turning his face to see his profile, "second cousins, twice removed."

Delia was happy to hear her dinner guests laugh and continue to conjecture about how distant their relationship might be.

Orrin and Larry, related or not, had a good deal more in common than many blood relatives have. At dinner they touched on many diverse subjects and found that they held similar views. On things political and social, they were in total agreement.

Later, over coffee in the den, they traded observations and opinions about the people in the world of advertising whom they both knew. Again, they were in accord as to who were and were not "horses' asses."

From a vantage point across the room, Delia watched with pride as her nephew and her abductee enjoyed their cigars and each other's company.

The following day, Larry introduced Orrin to his girlfriend, Sandra, who found Orrin to be delightful and endearing. She dubbed him a "Four-H" man—"happy, humorous, handsome, and hard to resist."

At the wedding ceremony on the flowered back lawn of Delia's estate in South Hampton, Sandra was both happy and sad. Sad that the dynamics of her long friendship with Larry would, of necessity, be changing, and happy that Larry had chosen her to act as his best person at his and Orrin's wedding.

Delia felt that she had done something very special and allowed herself to weep openly as she accepted dozens of congratulations on her brilliant matchmaking. Among the well-wishers were her brother and sister-in-law, the beaming Mr. and Mrs. Sebastian West, who adored their son Larry's choice of mate, and the less pleased Republican congressman Wilbur Harte Tuttle who, only a week earlier, had learned of Orrin's sexual orientation. Three months after the ceremony, as a belated wedding present to his son and son-in-law, the congressman, with some prodding from his wife, voted aye on a comprehensive gay rights' amendment.

Dial 411
for Legal Smut

"HELLO, INFORMATION? I'd like to place an obscene phone call but I don't want to go beyond the bounds of good taste."

"Sir, you want a nine-hundred number."

"Oh, I don't want to talk obscenely to a stranger. The nine-hundred-number people are the ones who do that for a living, aren't they?"

"Yes, they are."

"Well, that won't do. I want to talk to my girlfriend."

"I see; well, then, I suggest you call her."

"I intend to, but how can I be certain that I won't be cut off for using unacceptable language?"

"I'm sure I don't know."

"Well, who does know?"

"I'll connect you with my supervisor."

———

"Yes, can I help you?"

"I hope so. I'd like to place an obscene phone call,

and I was wondering if you have a list of words or phrases that have been ruled obscene. I wouldn't want to run afoul of the law while chatting with my girl-friend."

"Well, sir, what do you intend to say to her?"

"Well, I dreamed of her crotch last night, and I'd like to tell her about it."

"I don't think there'll be a problem there."

"I'd also like to inform her that I would love to nurse on her breasts until she moans with ecstasy. Can I say 'breasts'?"

"'Breasts' is an acceptable word."

"Good. Then I'd like to say a few things about her vagina."

"Such as?"

"Oh, how I'd like to fondle it for a while . . ."

"I see no problem there."

"Oh good. Can I say 'cock'?"

"AT and T would prefer you say 'penis,' but, if we're not monitoring the context, 'cock' might be acceptable. You see, 'cock' could be referring to a male rooster."

"Oh, that's great. I want to use 'cock' a few times."

"Well, sir, I wouldn't overdo it if I were you."

"Are you speaking professionally or aesthetically?"

"Aesthetically. The word would lose its impact if it were overused."

"Oh, I wouldn't overuse it, but I feel that just saying it once wouldn't be as effective as repeating it four or five times, in sort of a rhythmic way, you know, like Vachel Lindsey's poem about the jungle."

"I see what you're getting at."

"Well, thank you, you've been a big help. I guess I'll just go ahead and make my obscene phone call."

"A word of caution, Mister, uh, did you say your name?"

"I don't think so. It's Gilbert, Gilbert Corona."

"Zina Hathaway here."

"How do you do, Mrs. Hathaway."

"*Miss* Hathaway. What I was saying, Mr. Corona . . . Corona, is that a Spanish name?"

"Yes, my father's family is from Argentina."

"Ah. As I was saying, Mr. Corona, if you're thinking of using words in addition to 'crotch,' 'vagina,' 'breast,' or 'cock' . . ."

"Well, I may. In the heat of conversation, other words might pop into my mind. I do know a lot of provocative words."

"In that case, Mr. Corona, it might be advisable to have them checked out."

"What words should I try to avoid?"

"There are so many of them . . ."

"For instance?"

"Well, offhand, 'prick' out of context, 'sucking' in some contexts . . . as I say, there are so many of them. I'd like to be more helpful, Mr. Corona, but I don't have the time right now. Look, why don't you call me later at

1-212-555-1123? I'll compile a comprehensive list of all the words and phrases that you should avoid using."

"What time shall I call?"

"Well, I leave here at five, and if traffic is normal, I'll be home at six."

"This is so nice of you, Miss Hathaway."

"I'm always happy to help someone who shows such sensitivity. I'll expect your call at six. That's 1-212-555-1123. If I'm not home by that time, just keep calling back until I pick up. Do you have a redial feature?"

"I do."

"Good. Until six . . . *Gilberto.*"

How Could This Happen?

WHAT HAD he done? Was he being punished for his sins? What sins? He had always lived according to the rules, he had toed the line, done to others as he wanted them to do to him. Was he being singled out, or was this horror also being visited on others? He was afraid to move. A sharp pang of hunger stabbed at his gut. Bread, a tiny, tiny crust of bread was all he needed, or a drop of water, but where would he find either? Maybe under the kitchen table, but how would he get to the kitchen? He was flat on his back, something he always dreaded might happen to him. He strained to raise his head but couldn't. He felt strangely disconnected. He had no feeling in his legs. He looked down his body to see them. What had happened to his legs? Oh god! Most of them were gone; only two were left, and what a strange shape they had taken! It was imperative that he get off his back and find his family. With a herculean effort he rolled over and landed on the floor. The kitchen! He must try to crawl into the kitchen. But how could he crawl anywhere with just two legs? He strained and strained and finally pulled himself upright. He looked toward the kitchen and took heart. There was his whole family, crawling toward him!

Dozens and dozens of his siblings encircled him, warily keeping their distance. They seemed to be so small and so far away. Finally, his mother or his father, he was never able to tell one from the other, scurried up the leg of the kitchen table and stared up at him.

"Mom, or Dad, what has happened to me?"

"My son," one of them chirped, "you are no longer one of us."

"Oh dear god, tell me, what am I?"

"Gregor, darling," the other parent cried, "you have turned into a . . . a Kafka!"

Mr. Gutman
and Dr. Magic

"SIR, IS THIS some kind of gimmick?"

"I assure you, it isn't, Mister . . . ?"

"Gutman."

"Mr. Gutman, there is no gimmick to my offer."

"It sure sounds gimmicky."

"What sounds gimicky?"

"Well, for one thing, your name, Dr. Magic."

"It's my professional name. What else sounds gimmicky?"

"The offer itself. You guarantee an awful lot of things for three hundred dollars."

"Two hundred ninety-nine dollars."

"Who're you trying to fool? Why not just make it three hundred?"

"Because what I offer is worth two hundred and ninety-nine dollars and not a penny more!"

"How do I use this stuff?"

"It all depends on what you want it to do, Mr. Gutman."

"Let's say, Doc, that I'm interested in everything you claim it can do."

"I thought you might be. All right, get a pencil and paper and write down what I tell you."

"Isn't there a brochure?"

"If I had brochures printed, it would bring the cost up. Ready?"

"I guess. Shoot."

"Well, for baldness you take a tablespoonful every day with meals and, before retiring, massage a tablespoonful of it into your scalp. For lower back pain, rub a teaspoonful of the formula into the troubled area. For hearing loss, one drop in each ear daily. For a sinus condition, two drops in each nostril on awakening. For jock itch and athlete's foot, a half cupful added to your washing machine rinse cycle. For constipation, one tablespoonful stirred into your morning juice, unless you're also treating your baldness, in which case just add a quarter teaspoonful to your morning baldness dose. For dry, itchy skin, three capfuls dropped into your warm bath. For lip herpes, dip a Q-Tip into the formula and apply gently to the sore every hour for six hours and repeat the following day. For failing eyesight, one drop in each eye daily until the condition reverses itself. For hemorrhoids, apply directly to the swelling with a soaked cotton ball and hold there until relief comes, usually within six to nine minutes. Now, Mr. Gutman, this formula will not cure venereal disease, cancer, Parkinson's, or AIDS, and I'd be a fraud if I told you it would."

"I'll take it."

"You won't be sorry, Mr. Gutman."

"What if I need a refill?"

"You'll never need one. This gallon will permanently cure all the illnesses I've enumerated."

"What if I'm not satisfied?"

"Mr. Gutman, only a malcontent would not be satisfied."

"I am a malcontent."

"A malcontent? Really? Hmmm. Mr. Gutman, why don't you try taking a small gulp of my formula right now."

Mr. Gutman swallowed a dose of the magic elixir and waited expectantly.

"So, Mr. Gutman, what's the verdict?"

"It works!" he announced gleefully, handing Dr. Magic a check. "I'm so pleased!"

"Hold on, Gutman! A dollar more, please!"

"But you said two hundred and ninety-nine . . ."

"Yes, but that was before I discovered my formula would cure malcontentment."

Mr. Gutman was more than happy to pay the extra dollar.

The People Versus De Marco

"STATE your name."

"Anthony De Marco, Your Honor."

"Are you represented by counsel?"

"I'm gonna be my own counsel."

"How do you plead?"

"Well, I don't know. What's better, guilty with an explanation or not guilty with no explanation?"

"Are you sure you don't want the advice of counsel? The court can appoint one."

"No, I'll be all right. I'm gonna plead guilty with an explanation. What I did is perfectly understandable if you know the circumstances. Even you, Judge, would have done what I did."

"May we hear what you did?"

"Certainly, Your Honor, that's what we're here for, right?"

"Right, Mr. De Marco. Continue."

"A little justice tempered with mercy, that's all I'm asking for."

"We'll try to accommodate you."

"Thank you, Your Honor. Well, what happened was this. Last night, about midnight, I hear a scream that knocked me out of my bed. It's like no scream I ever heard before, a real bloodcurdler, like in a slasher movie. Anyway, I pick myself off the floor, and I'm looking at my girlfriend, Viola, who lives with me—we're engaged, by the way. She's yelling at the top of her lungs and pointing to the window. I run to the window and look out, and there's nothing there but a big moon and some trees. She keeps screaming and pointing, so I grab her by the shoulders and shake her but she just keeps hollering and pointing, so I do what anybody would do to bring her out of it, I give her a whack on the cheek."

"Hard enough to cause the abrasions that are described in the police report?"

"Oh, no way, Your Honor. I used an open hand. Her cheek wasn't even red. Anyway, she starts blubbering that she was attacked by a big bat."

"A big bat, Mr. De Marco?"

"I knew you'd be dubious. Yeah, a big bat, Your Honor, she said it looked like Dracula. I tell her she had a nightmare, but she keeps insisting that Dracula was in the room and he bit her, and she's afraid he'll come back and bite her again. She says that if he bites you a couple of times, you turn into a vampire. I tell her she's nuts, but she shows me her neck, and you know what, Your Honor?"

"Nooo, tell me!"

"There's, like, two small hickeys there. I tell her it wasn't Dracula that bit her but one of Spunky's fleas. Her dog, Spunky, sleeps with us. She gets real insulted and screams, 'I just gave him his flea bath!' 'Maybe you missed a couple,' I yell back."

"Mr. De Marco, where is this story going?"

"Right to the truth, Your Honor. Shall I continue?"

"Please do."

"Well, with the help of a triple dose of NyQuil and a couple of lullabies—I'm a singer, you know."

"No, I didn't, Mr. De Marco."

"I go by the name of Val Valino. I did a couple of commercials for Valvoline motor oil. That's where I got my stage name, Val Valino."

"Can we get back to your explanation, Mr. De Marco?"

"Right, Your Honor. I'll try to make it fast. I know you got a lot of criminals waiting in the bull pen. So, there we are, sound asleep, and I wake up to take a leak—is it all right to say that? I don't mean no disrespect."

"None taken, please continue."

"Thank you, Your Honor. So I'm coming back from the crapper and am I in for a surprise. This damned Dracula that Viola's been screaming about, you're not going to believe this, Your Honor, but there he is, hovering over our bed."

"You're right, Mr. De Marco, I don't believe it."

"I told you you wouldn't. I don't blame you for being skeptical. I never believed in vampires either, but I'm a believer now. I tell you, I went berserk. This Dracula guy is about to give my Viola another one of his famous vampire bites, and I'm scared she's going to get sucked into his world, so I grab my baseball bat—you know I used to play on the Valvoline company team . . ."

"No, I didn't."

"Oh yeah, left field. I'll tell you about that later. Anyway, I swing from the heels, and I clip this SOB right in the chops and he takes off like a big-assed bird, right out the window. I think I knocked out one of his fangs. Unluckily, on my follow-through, the bat clipped Viola on her cheek and that's how she ends up in the hospital with those abrasions you got there in the police report. Well, that's it, Your Honor. That's why I pled guilty with an explanation."

"And *that* is your explanation?"

"Yes, Your Honor. No good?"

"Unless you have a better one, Mr. De Marco, I'm afraid we're going to have to arraign you."

"Okay, how about this one? I'm at work and I start to get these flu symptoms, you know, aches and fever, so I go home early and find Viola taking a shower with my cousin Carmine. He's singing 'April Showers' and soaping her up and she's laughing and having a wonderful time, and when they see me, you know what they do, Your Honor?"

"I'm counting on you to tell me, Mr. De Marco."

"Nothing. They don't do nothing. Carmine just keeps on soaping and singing and Viola keeps on laughing. They invite me in. They're shameless. I don't know if it was the flu or the hot steam from the shower, but I could feel my blood boiling. I had to do something. So, I open the shower door, and yank them out of there. . . . That's all I did. Your Honor, I know you're wondering how Viola got those bruises you saw."

"You've read my mind."

"Well, they were both soaped up, and when they stepped onto the tile floor, they slipped and went flying. On her way down, Viola hit her cheek on the towel rack and Carmine fell right on my fist—I admit it was clenched, and lucky it was there or he would have crashed into the toilet bowl. You like that explanation any better, Your Honor?"

"A little. How accurate is it?"

"Very . . . except for a few details, Your Honor."

"I'd appreciate hearing those few details."

"Well, I ordered both of them out of my house, and while they were getting dressed, I lectured them on loyalty and trust, and I emphasized my disappointment in their behavior."

"How did you do that?"

"By whacking them with my nephew's Wiffle ball bat. Lucky for them my Louisville slugger wasn't handy. I tell you, Judge, I was boiling. Truth is, I'm still pretty hot."

"In that case, Mr. De Marco, to help you cool off I'm giving you ninety days in the county jail."

"Good idea, Judge, but I could cool off in thirty."

"I'd prefer you use the full ninety."

"Then ninety it is! You're the judge."

"Thank you, Mr. De Marco."

"Any time!"

Too Damned Handsome

DINO ROMANO did not stand a chance. His mother was a Victoria's Secret model and his father, who died in a demolition derby in Hackensack six months before he was born, was once described as a handsome version of Robert Redford.

Lying in his carriage, Dino heard, but never understood, the hundreds of compliments that came his way.

"Mrs. Romano," neighbors and strangers cooed, "that is the most beautiful baby I have ever seen in my life."

In the park, when he was old enough to play in the sandbox, he began to sense that something was going on that involved him.

Dozens of times he heard people say to his mother, "Madam, I have seen gorgeous children in my life, but your little girl is really out-of-this-world gorgeous!"

Informed that Dino was a boy, they would shake their heads in disbelief. One woman asked, "Are you sure?"

As a child, he was too pretty to be a boy and as a teenager he was too pretty to be a man. His eyelashes were the envy of every mooning female who had ever stared into his lavender eyes.

His football teammates nicknamed him Liz. Being blond, he never thought he looked like Elizabeth Taylor until she bleached her hair for a movie role. At that point he was tempted to dye his hair black.

All through high school and his one semester in a trade school, he was urged to become an actor, or at least a model.

"A male model or a female model," a cruel friend suggested, "you'd never be out of work."

By the time he was twenty-three, he had tried everything and failed miserably at each endeavor.

While Mother Nature had blessed him with extraordinary looks, she thought to balance the scale by giving him no discernible talent or personality, and just enough intelligence to allow him to experience frustration, pain, and anger.

Why, he asked himself, does everybody expect so much of me just because I'm so goddamned handsome?

He had lived up to his potential, but no one would accept that. Dozens of girls fell in love with him on sight, and all were disappointed to learn that he was not only content driving a beer truck but actually enjoyed the work. After too many years of failing to live up to his looks, he decided that he'd had it.

He didn't ask to be born with devastatingly handsome features and he was not going to accept his fate a day longer. One afternoon, after being told by a salesgirl that he was "soooo, soooo beautiful," he grabbed a phone book and randomly chose one of the dozens of plastic surgeons listed in the Beverly Hills yellow pages.

"Dr. Cutler," he pleaded, "what can you do for me?"

The doctor examined a face that he had tried many times to sculpt onto his needier patients.

"Unless you're running from the law," the doctor said, shaking his head, "why would you want to change your face?"

"It doesn't go with my personality."

"Well, then, I suggest you try changing your personality because your face is perfection and I never tamper with perfection."

When Dino asked Dr. Cutler if he could recommend someone who might be willing to help him, the doctor angered him by recommending a psychiatrist.

He visited every plastic surgeon listed in the yellow pages, and all had similar reasons for rejecting his business. He was shocked and disappointed to learn that there were so many ethical doctors in the profession. He became so depressed that he found it difficult to get out of bed. One morning he called in sick and told his supervisor that he would not be coming to work for a while.

His depression made it impossible for him to function. One afternoon he stood stock-still in the parking lot of a mini-mall, unable to decide where to lunch. For fifteen minutes he vacillated between Tico Tico Tacos and Korean Barbecue and finally decided on Korean Barbecue only to learn that it had gone out of business. Nothing was going his way. There was a long line of people waiting to be served at Tico Tico Tacos so he settled for two of Winchell's doughnuts and a cup of coffee.

He sat at a red plastic table on a yellow plastic chair and bit into his doughnut, looking at where Korean Barbecue had been. He noticed a shiny brass plaque on the door and wondered what was written there. He picked up his coffee and went to investigate. He smiled when he discovered that Korean Barbecue was now the Plastic Surgery Institute of Southern California. On the stucco wall beside the door were two smaller brass plaques with the names Dr. C. Hasegawa and Dr. H. Hasegawa. They weren't listed in the yellow pages, he thought. Hmmm, maybe they're not so damned ethical as the ones who are listed.

With doughnut in hand, he entered the offices of the Doctors Hasegawa and asked the receptionist if he might see either of the them. She informed him that they were both available and that he could see either of them. To avoid having to tell his story twice and being rejected twice, he asked to see both doctors at the same time.

The Doctors Hasegawa were short men and wore identical large-frame glasses. On the office walls hung many impressive-looking university diplomas in both English and Japanese. Displayed on their desks were framed photographs of their plain but pleasant-looking wives and children.

Dino explained to the Doctors Hasegawa what his problem was but did not tell them that he had been rejected by dozens of plastic surgeons. They examined Dino's face, consulted for a few minutes in Japanese, and, taking into account how tortured the man seemed to be, decided to help him.

The following day, at the Plastic Surgery Institute of California in a Vermont Avenue mini-mall, the Doctors Hasegawa performed a five-hour surgical procedure on Dino Romano's face. The doctors told him that all had gone well with the surgery and that they hoped he would be pleased with the results.

When the bandages were removed, Dino looked at himself in the mirror and was shocked but not disappointed by what he saw. He thanked the Doctors Hasegawa profusely for a job well done. All were happy—Dino, because he no longer looked like the annoyingly handsome man he had never wanted to be, and the doctors because they had taken a man with quite ordinary Occidental features and given him extraordinarily attractive Asian ones, features they themselves would love to have had.

After the swelling had gone and the bruises healed, Dino dyed his hair jet black and ventured out into the world. He discovered quickly that plastic surgery was not the solution. The operation had done nothing but add more Asians to his band of adoring women.

Without really comprehending why, four or five times a week he found himself on Ventura Boulevard lunching at Sushi Heaven. He had always liked Japanese food, but at Sushi Heaven he became intrigued with Mika, a demure Japanese waitress who seemed to look at him differently than most women did. So differently that, one day, he asked her why she kept staring at him. She apologized profusely and then, being uncharacteristically forward, asked if she might ask him a personal question.

"Shoot!" Dino answered.

"You have very nice black hair, sir, and I wondered why you dye your roots blond?"

There was something about Mika that made Dino want to tell her his life's story and he did, at the end of which she looked at him quizzically and shook her head.

"I don't think you are so handsome," she said softly.

"You don't?" he asked suspiciously. "You're not just saying that?"

"No," she said, smiling and looking into his eyes, "but you seem to be a nice person. Very sensitive . . ."

Dino spent the rest of the day driving his truck at half speed and thinking about dear, sweet-faced Mika. Did she really think he was not that handsome, and did she really think he was a nice person . . . and sensitive?

That evening, Dino returned to Sushi Heaven and ate the equivalent of two dinners while waiting for Mika to finish work.

At ten o'clock, over a cup of green tea, Dino told

Mika, "I like you, a lot," adding, "Since I told you all about myself, I think it's only fair that you tell me about yourself . . ."

At midnight, when the restaurant closed, Dino offered to drive Mika home and she accepted. He thought of calling a cab but decided that he would gamble that she liked him well enough to ride with him in a two-ton beer truck.

"A beer truck?" she screeched. "You're taking me home in a beer truck?"

"I just thought," he said apologetically, "that'd be fun for you."

"Fun?" she squealed.

"Well, I thought—"

"I am so excited. In Japan my father drove a truck. The best memories I have are of him driving me to school in his big Sapporo beer truck."

After saying good night to Mika, Dino said, again, "I like you, a lot," this time adding, "a whole lot . . ."

Xavier

ONCE XAVIER COBBLER made up his mind to do something, he would take a deep breath and inevitably decide to do something else. Once deciding to do something else, nothing could stop him from considering an alternate activity.

Today Xavier zeroed in on a most exciting project, rolled up his sleeves, and noticed a smudge of dirt on his forearm, which he took to the sink so he could wash the smudge away.

There was something about running water that started his mind whirring. So many of his most creative schemes had come to him in the shower or while he was urinating. As he scrubbed away at the stubborn Magic Marker stain on his arm, a new undertaking started to take form and it excited him. Nothing in the world could dissuade him from seeing this work to completion unless there was a major sporting event on television. He found one, the state bowling championship, live from Raleigh, North Carolina.

As he watched the bowling ball roll down the lane and strike the pins, he jumped up and shouted, "I've got it!" And he did have it, an idea for a great new board game— Procrastination!

He raced to the telephone, snatched it off the cradle, and punched in 411.

"The telephone number for the Milton Bradley company, please?"

Xavier was starting to dial the Bradley number when he remembered his ten o'clock appointment with Dr. Brunch.

Sitting in his psychiatrist's waiting room, Xavier fiddled with the slip of paper on which he had jotted down the phone number of the Milton Bradley company.

"417-555-1141," he mused, "split in two's would become 41-75-55-11-41, which I have a strong hunch are the winning numbers for tomorrow's Powerball lottery." He checked his watch and realized that if he rushed, he would have just enough time to buy a ticket before the lottery machines were shut down.

Bolting from the waiting room he pledged that, starting tomorrow, he would spend all of his time and energy working with Dr. Brunch on getting to the root cause of his problem with procrastination.

The following night Xavier watched the evening news and learned that his hunch was right, 41-75-55-11-41 were the winning numbers and the payoff was fifty-six million dollars.

"Fifty-six million dollars!" he mumbled over and over.

Xavier, who did not consider himself a religious man, clasped his hands in prayer and fell to his knees.

"Lord," he said, looking heavenward, "from this day forward, when I am on my way to buy a lottery ticket, I vow never again to stop at a Subway and wait in line to buy a tuna sandwich . . . unless I am really, *really* hungry."

Sorry Solomon and Guey Jew

SOLOMON BORENSTEIN decided to go to Chinatown. He had never ventured there in all the years he had lived in New York. Bertha loved Chinese food, but worried that the long subway ride from the Bronx would make her too queasy to enjoy the meal and always opted to stay in their neighborhood and eat Chinks. "Chinks" was the word they used until their son Paul convinced them that it was chauvinistic to use that word to describe either the Chinese people or their food. Bertha accepted her socially conscious son's advice and asked if it was racially kosher to order "pan-fried *luchshen?*"

Bertha could always get a laugh from her friends when she called Chinese noodles *luchshen*. It was eighteen months since Bertha had fainted at their traditional Sunday night dinner at the Empress of China. When she came to, she blamed the incident on the amount of Won Ton soup she had eaten. "God punished me for ordering it with the pork," she explained to Dr. Silver, who had rushed her to the hospital. Dr. Silver loved Bertha's humor, and he meant it when he called her "my best patient." Never once after she had been told that she had inoperable cancer did she blame any of her considerable discomfort on her condition. "I refuse to give those *fakahktah* germs power over my life!" she would declare.

Since her death, not one day went by without Solomon thinking of Bertha, and not one night that he did not long to hear her voice plead, "Solly, turn off the light already and go to sleep."

He had always preferred reading to sleeping, but reading had lost its allure and sleeping brought with it terror. Awake, he could control the agenda and choose to remember the pleasant experiences he and Bertha had shared in their fifty-eight years together. Asleep, he was at the mercy of a nonthinking brain that seemed to revel in replaying over and over again the fiery explosion in the Korean minefield where their only son, Paul, had been blown to his death. Many nights Solomon opted not to go to bed and would sit in front of the television set searching for any acceptable distraction.

The previous night, he watched the original *King Kong,* and it seemed to calm him. He had seen it many times and knew most of the dialogue by heart. He had amused his wife by turning off the sound and reciting the actors' lines. Bertha would laugh, hearing Robert Armstrong speak with a Russian-Yiddish accent.

Solomon's decision to go to Chinatown was inspired by

a PBS documentary he had seen that afternoon, "Life in New York's Asian Community." The bustling hordes of shoppers in the marketplace fascinated him. He was particularly drawn to the activity in the live chicken market.

In earlier times, when business was off and his boss found it necessary to give him an unpaid vacation, Solomon would accompany Bertha on her weekly pilgrimage to the live chicken market on Bathgate Avenue and help her select a bird for their Friday night boiled chicken dinner. The Bathgate Avenue he and Bertha knew no longer existed, and he wondered if going to Chinatown might help him to recapture some of the sounds and smells he had once complained about but now missed. Perhaps there he would find the spirit of Bertha and peace . . . and if not, he could buy a chicken and make a nice chicken soup for his Friday night dinner.

Although he had slept very little that night, he felt strangely energized. He and his Bertha were going to Chinatown to shop for a chicken and he would go by taxi. Bertha and Solomon rarely used taxis except for formal affairs when Bertha felt she was "too *fapitzed*" to ride the IRT. Well, she was not overdressed now, for he imagined her wearing one of the everyday flowered housedresses she had bought on sale at Klein's-on-the-Square.

He described to his driver the live chicken market he had seen in the documentary and asked if he could find it. Assured that it would be "no problema," Solomon settled back in his seat and closed his eyes, the better to imagine Bertha sitting beside him. He could hear her voice instructing the Puerto Rican driver on which route to take and how fast he should drive. He was shocked when he heard the cabbie say, "You the boss," but quickly realized that he had verbalized Bertha's instructions. She had spoken through him and it both frightened and delighted him. The driver actually said, "You the boss!" Those were the words Bertha had always used when she gave him an instruction that he was reluctant to carry out.

For a moment he considered that he might be possessed by her spirit. "Oy," he muttered, "Maybe I should go find an exorcist."

"You want me to look for an exercise place?" the driver asked.

"No, no," Solomon laughed, "don't listen to me. I was talking to myself. You take me to the chicken market."

Settling in his seat, he thought of how Bertha would have roared at the image of her Solly going to an exercise class. For the first time since Bertha's passing eighteen months before, Solomon felt at peace. He closed his eyes and rested his head on his hand. Images from the documentary projected themselves on his eyelids. He saw again the old wizened Chinese shopkeeper standing patiently amid dozens of crates of squawking hens while Chinese housewives searched for the perfect chicken.

Bertha could be one of them, he thought, and she

would have loved the shopkeeper. She had a special rapport with all people, from their neighbors, to the women who did housework for her twice a week, to the waiters she kidded with in restaurants.

As Solomon nodded off, images from the documentary and memories from his life intertwined. The Confucius-resembling chicken store owner, walking with Bertha on Bathgate Avenue, having Sunday dinner with their young son at the Empress of China. His reverie was shut down abruptly by the voice of his driver asking, "Mister, is this the chicken market you saw on the TV?"

Ignoring his arthritic back, Solomon jumped out of the cab, paid the driver, and added one of the largest tips he had given anyone.

"Who are you? Mr. Rockefeller? A thirty percent tip you give?" he heard Bertha admonishing. "Are you *meshugah*?"

"No, I'm not crazy," Solomon shouted to the voice in his head. "I just feel good."

The driver smiled, accepted the old Jew's pronouncement that he was not crazy, and drove off.

Solomon stood at the curb and stared at the hundreds of brown-and-white leghorns imprisoned in wooden crates, the curious ones jerkily pushing their silly little heads between the slats and then hastily withdrawing them, as if frightened by what they had seen.

They had a right to be frightened, he thought, but why was he suddenly fearful? They're the ones who are going to have their heads chopped off. You came here of your own free will.

He now questioned himself as Bertha might. "Why did you travel all these miles from the Bronx, and in a cab yet? What do you expect to find here?" Bertha was right. He was *meshugah*. He was looking for peace. Did he think he would find it here in this poultry death row with its screeching inmates? As he turned to look for a way back to the Bronx, he heard a strange voice speaking a strange language, and it seemed to be addressing him. He turned back and there before him stood the poultry shop owner he had seen in the documentary. Solomon suddenly found himself behaving as a fan might on meeting a movie star.

"Hey, mister," Solomon blurted out, "I saw you on the television last night with your chickens."

The old man cocked his head and squinted at Solomon.

"On the documentary about Chinatown," Solomon explained. "I saw you grab that screaming chicken that was flapping its wings and talk to it in Chinese. I don't know what you said, but the bird calmed down, and then you sold it to a lady. "

The man stroked his long, wispy beard and did not react to what Solomon was saying, but continued staring at him.

"The TV show," Solomon explained, speaking slowly. "I saw you on the TV."

"Sorry!" the old man blurted out, pointing his gnarled finger at Solomon, "Sorry!"

"For what?" Solomon asked. "It was a good show."

Screwing up his wrinkled face, the old man pointed again at Solomon and repeated, "Sorry! Sorry," and then, pointing to himself, nodded and said what sounded like "Jew, Jew!"

Solomon wondered what the bent old man had done that needed an apology and why he called himself a Jew. Solomon shook his head and tried to communicate in words and pantomime that there was no need to apologize. As Solomon spoke, the old man became more and more agitated and started to shout at him in a language he didn't recognize. It wasn't Chinese and it wasn't English. The more perplexed Solomon became, the louder the little man shouted. The veins in his temples were filling to the bursting point when Solomon, fearful for the old man's life, grabbed him by the shoulders and suggested that he compose himself. The man did, then slowly repeated what he had been saying. On hearing these same words spoken calmly, Solomon suddenly understood that the Chinese gentleman was not apologizing to him. He wasn't saying sorry, he was saying Solly, Bertha's nickname for him.

"Sorry," the old Cantonese gentleman asked again, "*du vilst luchshen mit dein won ton soup?*"

"No, no," Solly guffawed, "I don't want noodles with my won ton soup."

Du vilst luchshen mit dein won ton soup was one of the many Yiddish phrases Bertha had taught this man eons ago when he had worked as a waiter at the Empress of China. On learning that his name was Guey Jew, Bertha had insisted on teaching him a few choice Yiddish phrases.

"Guey Jew!" Bertha advised him, "With that name you should know a few Yiddish words in case you get a job in a kosher deli."

The two men looked into each other's moist, red-rimmed eyes. Solomon wondered if Chinese people hugged and then remembered that this one did. When Guey had mastered a particularly difficult Yiddish phrase, Bertha would reward her pupil with a hug and a blessing; "*A leiben uff dein cupf,* Mr. Jew!" It was obvious to Solomon that a good life had been visited upon Guey Jew's head.

"So, Sorry," Guey ventured, releasing himself from Solly's grasp, "*vos macht a Yid?*"

"The Jew is doing fine," Solomon chuckled and before he could censor himself asked, "*Vos macht a* Chink?"

"The Chink *macht a leiben.*" Guey laughed, adding, "A better living than I make as waiter in Bronx."

While Guey's son plucked and dressed the chicken they had both agreed was the plumpest and tenderest of all, the two old acquaintances chatted amiably about their lives as widowers.

"Hey, Sorry," Guey called out as Solomon climbed into a taxi, "*gay kahken offen Yom?*"

"Guey, do you know what you just said to me?"

"Go in good health?"

"No, you just told me to go shit in the ocean."

"I getting old. I forget my Yiddish," Guey said, laughing. "What is other *gay* that mean 'Go with health'? Gay eight zinter?"

"Almost. It's *Gay gahzinteraight.*"

"That's it," Guey chuckled, shutting the cab door. "*Gay gahzinteraight*, Sorry."

That afternoon, with Bertha's voice guiding him through the process, Solly filled the old cast-aluminum pot with cold water, threw in a scrubbed chicken, a large carrot, a big brown onion, two stalks of celery, and a parsnip. Miraculously, he duplicated the delicious boiled chicken dinner that Bertha had served every Friday night of their lives.

Solomon slept well that night.

The Almighty
New Information

I KNOW fifteen things about God that are never mentioned anywhere:

He has a chronic back condition.

His knee joints ache.

He is allergic to shellfish and mustard.

His prostate is moderately enlarged.

He sings off-key.

He hates wars but can't think of a way to stop them.

He loves to check out a woman's legs as she passes by.

He is upset at the unfair distribution of wealth.

He loves to laugh.

He gets goose bumps when a great tenor hits a high C.

He hates that comedies never win Oscars.

He loves sushi, especially unagi.

He hates talking to anyone wearing a tongue ring.

He loves Fred Astaire.

He would like to replace the TEN COMMANDMENTS with the ONE COMMANDMENT that covers everything: "THOU SHALT NOT HURT ANYBODY!"

How do *I* know these things about God?
I am *man*, and *I* was created in His image.